MAD
AS HELL

MAD
AS HELL

America's #1 All-Night Radio Host
Takes on the Dangerous World We Live In

GEORGE NOORY

A Tom Doherty Associates Book
New York

*I dedicate this book to my mother, Georgette,
who has helped shape and guide me all my life,
and to my amazing children, Wendy, Kristina, and Jonathan,
who made parenting look easy!*

Acknowledgments

I'd like to acknowledge my editor, Bob Gleason, and my associate editor, Elayne Becker, at my publisher Tor/Forge for the remarkable support on all my projects, and the late Guy Gibson who helped mold me into the broadcaster I am today.

Contents

Author's Note

From the City of Angels off the Pacific Ocean, good morning, good evening, wherever you may be, across the nation, around the world. I'm George Noory. Welcome to America's most listened-to late-night talk show, *Coast to Coast AM*.

INTRODUCTION

Strangers in a Strange Land

We live in a dangerous world that has been changing at warp speed, making it hard to keep one's footing.

We are going through a metamorphic process, changing, transforming as a planet, a nation, a people, and a society.

Some of the changes are shaped by history and natural events in our physical environment, including the incredible transformation of technology over the past several decades.

Above all, we live in a dangerous world that is spinning out of control. We are confronted by endless wars, terrorism, global instability, and environmental disasters that are often suspiciously "not natural."

The metamorphosis is not just about things but about *people*—you and me and our neighbors and families across the street, across the nation, and around the world.

As a national radio host with my ear to people who reflect a cross section of our nation, I see folks being stretched mentally, emotionally, the planet being divided into a tiny group of privileged haves and a vast number of have-nots while the middle class is steadily losing what it worked so hard for.

Somewhere along the line we need to get back to a middle ground, because if we don't, our social order will burst at the seams.

My biggest concern, one that I am acutely aware of each

night that my show is broadcast coast to coast, is the frustration and tension of people with just about *everything*. There is anger and even rage on the part of some, gloom and a sense of doom in so many others.

I see myself not only as an entertainer but also as a facilitator trying to create calm in a very stressed world.

People are stressed because they don't know where they are headed in a world they seem to have no control over.

The world is changing faster than most of us can keep track of—it is so fast and slippery that a great number of people can't keep their footing.

Most of us feel puzzled by the events reshaping the world into a form radically different than the one we were born into. Puzzled and even alienated. We wonder where we came from, where we are going.

And who is pulling the strings.

I see premeditation and malice behind much of what is destabilizing the world, and the weakening of America as it is forced into being the world's policeman in endless conflicts around the globe. I see it in droughts that are driving up food prices and creating hunger; a billion people without access to pure drinking water; people being displaced globally, by the tens of millions, by war and climate change; terrorist nations, hordes from the Dark Ages, that suddenly arise *fully armed* with cutting-edge military weapons where there had been dust and rust before.

There are scheming hands controlling many of these machinations, intrigues to interconnect our nation with the rest of the world in order to make it easier to divide and conquer.

I see something else, too. The pale specter of biblical prophecies.

Before we discuss these things at greater length, I'd like to tell you a bit about myself and how I came to this knowledge.

PART I

I'M MAD AS HELL

We have ills in our society that make people feel helpless, while our political leaders fail to deal with problems that affect us. The cleansing we need of our political system, our border problems, the destruction of the middle class, the endless wars, and barbarians from the Dark Ages are changes akin to a "flood" of biblical proportions.

1

"I'm as mad as hell, and I'm not going to take this anymore!"

The line is from the 1976 movie *Network*. The statement has been immortalized by the American Film Institute as one of the greatest movie lines in history, along with such memorable ones as "Frankly, my dear, I don't give a damn," from *Gone with the Wind*, and "I'm going to make him an offer he can't refuse," from *The Godfather*.

The film is about a TV news anchorman, Howard Beale (played by the late Peter Finch), who is fighting a losing battle, struggling to accept the social ills and widespread corruptions in the world he reports upon for a television network. Finch delivers the line when he is on the air ranting about and lamenting the sad state of the world, which no one seems to be doing anything about.

Peter Finch won an Academy Award for his performance (as did two of the other actors and the screenwriter), and the film was selected by the National Film Registry for preservation in the Library of Congress, as "culturally, historically, or aesthetically significant." (A footnote to Finch's Academy Award: he passed away before learning he had won for Best Actor.)

You might wonder why I am bringing up this seventies flick. Or, as Howard Beale put it in the movie, "What has that got to do with the price of rice?"

I am mad for many of the same reasons Howard Beale was— the ills of today's world that most people feel helpless about are not that much different than those of the fictional world that sent Howard Beale into violent rants. The film reflects much about what's wrong with our own society and about the people who are supposed to be doing something about the problems.

What grates me the most is that the people we rely upon, the ones we elect because they promise to deal with the problems, that we give the money and the power to so the problems can be fixed, are too often lazy, corrupt, incompetent—or just don't care.

In the film, Beale says that everyone knows things are bad, that there's a depression, people are out of work or scared of losing their job, the air's unfit to breathe, the dollar's deflated, shopkeepers keep guns under the counter, "and we sit watching our TVs while some local newscaster tells us that today we had fifteen homicides and sixty-three violent crimes, as if that's the way it's supposed to be."

He believed that people should start changing the system by first getting mad.

Sound familiar? Maybe all the woes that bothered him aren't exactly the same as they are today in our society, but they are close enough. And they are just as solvable, if our politicians and government leaders would do the jobs that they are well paid to do, instead of doing little while enjoying the fruits of *our* labors.

People say we need a change in Washington. They're not talking about whatever political party happens to be in power at the moment but a change in which our country is governed efficiently and effectively instead of being an unmanageable bureaucracy that has collapsed under its own sheer weight.

We need new faces with good ideas, not the same old faces with the same old hackneyed game plans.

I believe the middle class is being eroded, being sold out for the sake of multinational corporations with globalist agendas. Part of this is being done through free trade agreements and outsourcing high-paying jobs offshore.

Our borders are so porous, so leaky, that we are flooded

with millions of immigrants who can become a burden on our resources—with the burden being shifted to the taxpayers.

I'm not about to give you a laundry list of everything that needs to be fixed in America, because it would take up more space than a set of the *Encyclopaedia Britannica*, but I do want to hit some high points that I have gleaned from experts, concerned callers, and my own experiences. I want to share some of my conclusions with you and hope that you will get as mad as I am and help me bring positive change.

2

A voice in the darkness.

I've been called a voice in the darkness for different reasons.

One reason is that my four-hour broadcasts are sent across a continent and oceans to millions during the graveyard hours. The show is listened to by people in all walks of life, from truck drivers barreling along dark highways to security guards in silent buildings and factories, to clerks stocking empty shelves in grocery and department stores, to others who are awake while most people are asleep and who want to share those quiet hours with me and those on my show.

I also have been unable to resist the impulse, the uncontrollable urge, to look into shadowy places few others have dared to enter. Since I was a child, I have been drawn to investigate mysteries, to seek answers about people, places, and things cloaked by shadow and fog. My natural inclination is to speak aloud thoughts and feelings about those dark places that many others share but are too frightened, out of fear or the threat of ridicule, to express.

Being a voice in the darkness begins with listening to other voices—voices that reflect the thoughts and observations of millions of my listeners. The primary talent of a good talk show host is not to love the sound of his or her own voice but to listen to what others want to share.

I hear from people in all walks of life, from every corner of North America and even from the Caribbean and the South Pacific.

Listening to so many others on the air and at events has given me what some people would call paranoia about certain aspects of our society. But I'm sure that most of us realize that oftentimes paranoia is actually a heightened awareness of what goes on around us. Or, as William S. Burroughs put it, sometimes paranoia is just having all the facts.

Hearing those late night voices, and from people at events where I am a speaker or moderator, I have also developed a heightened awareness that not everything about our world can be seen, explained, and categorized by science.

We'll get to that in a moment—miracles and ghosts and other things science can't find under a microscope—but first I want to talk about the physical world that surrounds us. There are hidden things all around us, events and situations in which most of us see only what the perpetrators want us to see. They are made invisible and incomprehensible by the deliberately perplexing and convoluted manipulations and intrigue that created them.

Looking deep into the darkness, into the blur of fog and shadow, I sense something about this dangerous world that we live in, about this planet that we call home and are trapped on, a situation still embryonic but growing. Without getting heavy into religion, which I tend not to do, I have come to the conclusion that we are in the early stages of the "end times" referred to in the Bible.

I am not saying that tomorrow there will be fire and brimstone from the heavens. With regard to the Book of Revelation, which talks about Armageddon, I believe we have entered that prophetic path of tribulation and adversity but are in the very early stages.

I have long-range views of the end times prophecies found in the New Testament and in other religious sources.

Again, without getting too biblical, we will get more into

end times and my own prophetic view of the events that signal it.

I will take you down some paths that may be unfamiliar—perhaps strange—even to those who have listened to my radio show.

3

Besides my end times prediction, I've also seen things looking in the darkness that even the most precise instruments of science can't see—if they even bothered to look.

Despite the belief of so many scientists that only what they can see on a petri dish in a lab is "real," God can't be found under a microscope—neither can love nor miracles nor evidence of the human spirit. And there are so many other things that science cannot see or, more often, simply refuses to investigate.

There is also an unwritten coercion of scientists that makes it necessary for them to reconcile and harmonize the results of their studies with the generally accepted paradigms of their calling. They fear that sticking their heads out of the box will result in their reputations getting whacked.

Scientists simply call what they cannot explain or will not attempt to explain "paranormal."

The paranormal is simply things that science does not have an explanation for; in general, these are matters science is not seeking answers about because it requires scientists to step out of the steel-walled cocoon in which all that they have seen and known has been provided.

Just as scientists fear scorn, airline pilots likewise refuse to report credible UFO sightings because they fear ridicule from others, even disciplinary actions from their employers.

Scientists share that same rocky road of condemnation when they dare to step out of the lockstep they have been molded to use since the first day they entered academia.

Intent listening for years, coupled with my experiences, my own "heightened awareness," and that of many other people, tells me that angels and spirits, miracles and UFOs, and many more of those things loosely categorized as "paranormal" do exist and have been experienced by many people.

My ears have become finely tuned to what people have actually experienced and what are lies, dreams, or hallucinations. It is impossible to spend years listening to voices coast to coast, to hear people share their experiences with ghosts and miracles, without realizing that there is more to the world than what is open and obvious.

I am a firm believer of Hamlet's point, made after Horatio heard Hamlet talking to the ghost of his dead father: *there are more things in heaven and earth than Horatio realized.*

Scientists need to get their heads out of their textbooks once in a while, put away their microscopes, and open their minds to the world around them—not just the world they can see with their instruments but also places from which they have turned their eyes and minds.

The inevitable conclusion I've reached is that all of us have the ability to sense more than what the eye sees, and that a few of us have worked to develop that sense to a high degree.

Later I'll relate a paranormal experience that I had when I was eleven years old. It was an experience that opened a door in my mind that permits me to look at the paranormal in a different way than most people. The curiosity that draws me to solve mysteries was stimulated by this event.

It's an area of human existence that most people also ignore out of fear of ridicule, because a scientist hasn't put a seal of approval on it.

Rather than ignore places in the darkness, I investigate them—matters as far ranging and provocative as the existence of spirits, ghosts, pesky poltergeists, and strange creatures grouped under the label of "cryptids"; extrasensory perception and telekine-

sis; life after death and reincarnation; faith healing, human au-
ras, and remote viewing; and the existence of other dimensions
and many other places that can't be seen under a microscope.

In a sense, I am always exploring those eternal questions:
Who are we? Where did we come from? Where are we going?

But we will be taking those cosmic questions up a notch
to include: Who are they? Where did they come from? Why are
they here?

It will be a wild ride, so hang on and join me.

Before I share with you my thoughts about the world today
and the future tomorrow, I need to talk a little about the show
that has brought so many people and ideas to me.

THE LISTENER

For four hours every night, on holidays and weekends, George Noory is the voice in the darkness for millions of Americans. His show, *Coast to Coast AM*, has perfected a charged and conspiratorial worldview that now pervades American media. It's quite possibly the oddest show ever to cross our airwaves. And it may change the radio business forever. . . .

Every night, when most of the world has drifted into unconsciousness, some 30 percent of the American population stays awake. They're truckers, insomniacs, night-shift workers, or just people who like to stay up late. . . . They tend to listen alone—alone in bed, alone on a highway, alone in the world—and find that a voice in the darkness offers a bond with a wider community. Perhaps you're one of them.

—Timothy Lavin, "The Listener,"
The Atlantic (2010)

4

It is midnight in Los Angeles, where I'm broadcasting; one o'clock in Denver; two in the morning in Dallas, from where "Norm" called in to the show to say he has been hearing from his deceased grandmother; three A.M. on the East Coast.

"My grandmother speaks to me," Norm tells me. "She died ten years ago and has just started speaking to me the past couple of months."

It's dark coast to coast, but Norm is awake, along with millions of other people, a surprising number of whom, like Norm, have experienced something science would say is outside its boundaries.

"Open lines" is the theme for tonight, a time when people can call in and talk about anything they wish to discuss. Sometimes we restrict calls to particular subjects, but tonight I let callers call the shots.

The call before Norm came from Diane in Helena, Montana. Diane talked about the Federal Reserve System, an outfit a lot of people find as scary as calls from the grave and alien abductions. Diane told me that the existence of the Fed violates the United States Constitution, that it has no oversight from Congress or the president, and that it operates in a financial shadow land in which its first priority is to look after the interests of banks rather than the public.

Because it is an important issue, and we have on the show expert guests who elaborate on matters of interest to our listeners, in the past we have had experts speak about the Fed—and many other subjects. One night it might be a NASA astrobiologist to explain the method being used by our government to search for life on other planets and star systems, an MIT astrophysicist on the investigation of dwarf black holes, or perhaps a couple of the top experts working to safeguard the fragile and easily damaged national power grid that our nation and national security rely upon 24/7, 365 days a year.

The night Norm called in about a ghost and Diane about the Fed, the guests could have been a ufologist analyzing a UFO sighting over Phoenix, a board-certified medical doctor and surgeon who believes that the medical profession must look for cures beyond the straitjacket confines of Western medicine, a leading authority on near-death experience, a man who has spent more than a decade tracking Bigfoot, or a speaker on just about any other subject of interest under the sun, moon, and stars.

Some of our expert guests are members of the inner circle of distinguished scientists and university professors whose written words appear frequently in science journals. We also stick our heads out of the box, asking what the other views are on a subject, and we seek intelligent and often world famous experts whose views conflict with what most others in the field embrace.

We keep our discussions about science, medicine, and other issues on the cutting edge, always asking what is here now and what is coming up.

We go deep with the scientists and other experts, often for hours, probing, questioning, seeking answers to questions that have never been properly tackled before.

We are just as attentive to the person who believes they have a guardian angel as we are to a forensic scientist who explains how DNA tests can give false results in criminal cases.

Our guests and callers include ordinary people who want to share an experience or have a question that can't be asked anywhere else and experts who are invited to share their research and conclusions—work that often doesn't have an outlet in their field of study because it deviates from the status quo.

We also approach major news items a bit differently than the rest of the media, offering a fresh take on a current news event rather than repeating the same information that people have been pounded with all day over TV and radio.

We explore and investigate subjects from different angles, analyzing the news rather than just mimicking what others are reporting.

As with callers and guests, the subject matter on the show is wide ranging. On any given night, we could have experts discussing the latest developments in weather modification, the newest Hubble and Kepler discoveries in the far reaches of the galaxy, the latest in the search for Bigfoot/Sasquatch in mountains and forests down here on terra firma, sensational techniques for recording messages from the dead through electronic voice phenomena, the coming collapse of the dollar and international monetary system, along with the approaching era when money will all be electronic—not to mention killer asteroids and alien abductions.

5

During a broadcast, I am at a desk with computer screens right and left and a TV on the wall. I am wearing earphones and facing a big mic. Sometimes I sit while we're broadcasting, other times I stand. The dress code is casual and so is the work atmosphere. I have been working with pretty much the same staff for over a decade. Everyone knows their job and they know it well.

Three main things are going on during the broadcast: our engineer is keeping us on the air, the producer and production staff are monitoring incoming calls, and I am talking to a guest or a caller.

Facing me, across the room, is my engineer. He's seated before banks of monitors that he uses to get us on the air and keep us there, occasionally passing me hand signals like a third-base coach.

In an adjoining room, with a glass partition so we can communicate with body language, is my producer and production assistant. This is where calls from our telephone lines come in.

The producer speaks to the caller, pretty much making sure that the caller can hold a conversation and is not inebriated. When we're discussing a particular subject, the producer is looking for callers able to communicate on the topic.

The call is passed to me by appearing on one of my computer monitors. The only information I am given about the caller is the person's first name and where they are calling from. The man hearing from his grandmother in the beyond would come through to me as simply "Norm—Dallas."

I don't want to be told what the caller is going to talk about because I want our discussion to be spontaneous. Keeping the calls natural and unrehearsed means no preparation by me or censoring of what will be said, although we don't allow profanity or other content prohibited by the Federal Communications Commission or by my own standards.

To ensure that unlawful content isn't broadcast, there is a forty-second delay in broadcasting, permitting us to use a fail-safe switch to delete prohibited remarks. Callers have to show respect for the audience.

The broadcast is carried by more than six hundred radio stations coast to coast plus Sirius XM's channel 146, north to Canada, over the Pacific to Guam, and down the Caribbean to the Virgin Islands. Much of it is transmitted over those tall towers we have all seen at night, the ones so high they have blinking lights to warn off airplanes. The broadcast also goes out over satellites and the Internet.

Monday through Friday, five nights a week, with guest hosts on the weekends. Four hours a night. The strange, the mysterious, and the bizarre—along with news about events in our dangerous world and cutting-edge science. There are no limits, except perhaps good taste.

I do prepare for guests. And if they have written a book, I make sure I'm familiar with it.

I work at being a good host for the audience, the callers, and the guests. As I mentioned earlier, being a good listener is my key to being a good host.

I keep an open mind and am nonjudgmental. I don't demand that someone who has heard from the dead bring me a recording of the conversation. I don't expect someone who says they have been abducted by extraterrestrials to bring me pictures of the captors.

As I said, like Hamlet, I know there are more things in heaven and earth than most of us have imagined or that science has found under a microscope.

Many of my callers are deeply affected and even traumatized by their experiences. Some have had a strange experience. Others need the space to express their fears about the state of the world.

Regardless of what is happening in people's lives (and often it is their fear of a changing world), they need empathy and an outlet to express themselves, rather than an intimidating shock jock shouting at them.

I provide a forum for people no one else will listen to. Along the way, I get priceless and fascinating information about the strange and the wonderful.

Besides the show five days a week, I head for Denver once a month and tape shows for an Internet TV program, and I frequently am doing the show at radio stations while doing speaking engagements around the country.

The "road" to *Coast to Coast* started in Detroit, when I was nineteen years old. It took a few decades, marriage, family, jobs at all levels of television and radio news, three Emmys, an adventure as a restaurateur, raising racehorses, some successes, and some failures (horse racing is called the sport of kings because horses eat and eat and eat).

I'll share with you the road I followed to where I am today, but right now I want to talk about the dangers I see we are facing. I will be saying some things many people won't like, that may even frighten some. But I will back up everything I have to say with facts and experience.

TALKING TO THE DEAD

On *Coast to Coast AM*, I deal with every paranormal, super-natural, spiritual, and mystical topic imaginable. There are no boundaries or limits, and both my guests and callers push the edges on any given night. Of all the subjects we hit on, the question of life after death ranks at the top. Most compelling of all are the frequent heartfelt testimonies of people who have been in contact with loved ones on the Other Side.

We have no scientific proof yet of the afterlife, but those who have had such experiences know deep within their hearts that the afterlife is real and that the people they love dearly are alive in that world.

—George Noory and Rosemary Ellen Guiley,
Talking to the Dead (2011)

6

We live in strange times. I'm sure few would disagree with that statement. There is not another time in history during which so many dangerous things globally occurred so quickly, changes coming at a speed never seen before, changes that affect every person in our nation and on the planet.

What has happened is that the interconnectivity of the Internet and the World Wide Web has linked billions of us together—bringing new meaning to that phrase "Misery loves company."

The biggest detriment of being connected with everyone and everything globally is that it creates a world easier for central control. When everyone is connected, it is easy to implement a One World Government, a One World Economy, and the natural result of all that is One World Control over all of us.

Looking at what is happening on every continent, the unusual path that war and terrorism, economic and climate disasters have taken, I see a silent hand stirring the pot.

As Sherlock Holmes said, the game's afoot, but this is a game in which we are pawns.

I tend to think that most of the events that have occurred have been premeditated—in other words, *deliberately created.*

Other outside influences besides the ones doing the manipulation get involved, to be sure, but there's something else afoot here, not a natural sequence of events but provocation and deliberation by powerful forces.

Uncommon events—sudden wars, antibiotic-resistant diseases, raging and often freaky weather, droughts and water short-ages, dangers to the power grid—have become more and more frequent, as if time and events are moving faster.

As the speed and frequency increases, the response by our government gets slower and drags.

We will examine what is afoot, including some of the calamities that affect society as seriously as the plagues God sent to punish the pharaoh.

Rather interestingly, those ten plagues in some ways mimic crises we are facing around the world, such as climate changes; drug-resistant diseases and pandemics; threats to turn our world dark by shutting down power grids; attacks on our vital food supplies by droughts, pests, and the disappearance of the bees we so depend upon.

It's not just events. People are mentally and morally evolving differently than what I've seen over most of my life. And they are doing it at a speed that leaves mere mortals unsettled.

Newsworthy events used to stand out to most of us. Today, people tell me that they have digitally "experienced" so many wars, atrocities, floods, famines, fire and brimstone that these events, earth-shattering to those physically involved, become a digital blur to those of us who experience them only on television or on our cell phones.

"Emotional innumeracy" is what psychiatrists call it when we become numb to tragedy.

All this goes back to my premise: there is control over what is happening. And before I am done, we will be pinning down where the control is coming from.

In order to achieve worldwide control, those manipulating the system would have to weaken the United States, because this country is the only one on the planet with both the power and the desire for true global peace.

America's patience, determination, and will to maintain

peace and sanity in the world is being tested every day, on every continent, by violence and upheaval, with natural resources diminishing around the globe to the point that future wars will be fought over drinkable water.

Let's take a look not at a "world war" but at a "world at war."

DEADENING THE PAIN:
EMOTIONAL INNUMERACY

Psychologists use the phrase "emotional innumeracy" to describe how the ability of people to empathize with disaster victims has become seriously limited.

A Duke University study, published in the *Journal of Experimental Social Psychology*, compared the reaction of people who read an article about the deaths of five people with the reaction of a group who read about the deaths of ten thousand. The findings showed no difference in emotion between those who read about five deaths and those who read about ten thousand. The conclusion reached was that we cannot make rational or emotional judgments about such a large number.

It reminds me of a quote commonly misattributed to Joseph Stalin: "One death is a tragedy; a million deaths is a statistic."

7

What I have heard and confirmed through my own investigations is that we live in a world that is becoming destabilized and that is in danger of spinning out of control—and that there is deliberation and premeditation behind it.

If you can destabilize the world, you have a world ready to be taken over, to divide and conquer.

Some of the danger comes from what is open and obvious about the world we see around us.

We live in an era in which hordes from the Dark Ages rise from small groups and grow like poisonous bacteria out of control, spread through fanaticism and reigns of terror, fueled by mass murder, terrorism, and torture. A single terrorist can intimidate a whole city by using mindless mass violence against helpless civilians, targeting busy streets, marketplaces, temples, churches, mosques, hotels, and tourist sites. They strike anywhere a small number of cowardly murderers can hurt as many innocent people as possible.

The incredible speed, rise, and transition of these global fanatics is mind-boggling. Over the past couple decades, a small group of terrorists who called themselves Al-Qaeda spread and created an environment for extremism in Syria and North and Central Africa. From what Al-Qaeda sowed, poisonous plants like the Islamic State of Iraq and the Levant (ISIL), Boko Haram, and others have popped up and delivered terror on two continents, with threats to take the violence global.

The brutal, macabre ISIL contagion that came to worldwide attention in 2014 is an example of a premeditated, deliberate, planned-in-advance event that seemed to come out of what appeared to be nowhere and was suddenly atop us like all of the plagues of Egypt hitting at once.

The strangest aspect of all is that terrorist armies are rising so suddenly, like ghosts in the desert, erupting out of the sands of the Middle East, one after another coming alive and suddenly attacking with tanks, armored vehicles, and the cutting edge of rifles, machine guns, grenade launchers, and other small arms.

When we start looking at how this terrorist movement appears to have evolved in a relatively short time, more questions than answers jump out at us: How did these people get so well-funded? How was a network instantly set up to sell hundreds of millions of dollars in stolen petroleum and to market the priceless relics of ancient civilizations that these maniacs are dismantling and selling—when they are not brutally destroying them?

Who bought them their new trucks and their Humvees and their SUVs?

Who armed them? Who gave them rifles and assault weapons and bullets and ammunition and all the food and supplies that armies need to march on?

Who's doing this?

Who got them organized so quickly, under the radar? They have organizational skills, money, uniforms, food, weapons, and propaganda tools. Where did it all come from?

Besides the logistical weapons and supplies, where did the fanatical will and the great, bottomless hate and mindless bloody rage come from?

Did some genie in a bottle wave a magic wand and, suddenly, demon armies marched from the pages of a book or off a movie screen?

I am being facetious, of course, but some of these cruel, murderous armies, with their Dark Ages mentality, appear similar to the demon armies created in fantasy novels and films, not to mention in biblical accounts.

Our government says, *Well, our military knew about this two years ago, when they warned us.* But if that was the case, no one told the public, because we didn't hear anything about it until it was a raging fire threatening many countries that we have taken the thankless job of protecting. That out-of-control fiery contagion will spread to our own country if we don't stop it and stamp it out.

ISIL's attack is just one example of a plague of wars that suddenly pop up. When this set of fanatics is crushed, there will be more stepping in to keep the evil flowing, because fanaticism is the only life that has meaning to these killers.

Killers are what they are. They are not people practicing a particular form of religion or politics, despite what they claim. They are killers, mass murderers who group together in packs like cowardly mad dogs.

8

The bloody brutal acts of terrorists and their endless atrocities so dominate our daily news that it tends to cloud a very pertinent fact about the dangers to our country: *we live in a world at war.*

At the time this is being written, there have been fifteen major conflicts in the past five years. Most of the wars were in Africa and the Middle East, although Asia had three and Europe had one (in Ukraine). That count does not include conflicts that are chronic, with violence erupting periodically for short spurts over long periods of time rather than battles that settle the disagreements.

Some of these conflicts have a religious basis. Some have been going on for so long that the reason for the violence gets glossed over and hate takes the place of other differences.

There are conflicts that have been going on for many decades. That includes Israelis and Arabs, and India and Pakistan, which are not counted among the fifteen mentioned. In addition, a civil war in Myanmar (formerly Burma), the Congo, and the on-again, off-again conflict between the Irish Republican Army and the British seems to be never ending.

Many of the conflicts that have become chronic have been going on for so long that most of the people in the world today were not even born when the violence started.

It makes one wonder what a visitor from another planet would think about the rationality and humanity of us earthlings.

What is in our face about all these wars is the daily violence and atrocities, but there is an underlying global tsunami that is also at work, destabilizing the world.

More than sixty million people have been violently displaced by conflicts, putting an incredible internal strain on these countries as well as strain on neighboring countries, on the United States, and on our allies. Tens of millions of people are homeless and lack adequate food, shelter, clothing, and medical aid. This is the largest number of people ever recorded as having been driven from their homes by the cruel winds of war. These people are the victims of terrorist armies, genocide, and wars that simply seem to have no beginning or end—wars that are just there, happening.

But there's something else afoot here besides the fighting and violence, the victims by the tens of millions, which we hear about on the news so often. There's a bigger picture for which I'm trying to put all of the pieces of the puzzle together. I believe one of my roles on *Coast to Coast* is to see what this puzzle looks like when we have the whole picture.

The pieces I have put together tell me that these endless, meaningless conflicts and the displacement of vast numbers of people, refugees by the tens of millions, is not an accidental consequence of wars fought over right or wrong but a result of wars that are premeditated, deliberate.

What I am grasping is that there is an end result to all these purposeful conflicts—a one-rule world government, created in order to break the United States down to nothing so that it can't defend itself, maintain peace in the world, or continue to police places that quickly go to hell in a handbasket. Not to mention that we are the world's major supplier of food and the world's major supplier of humanitarian aid.

I believe I'm useful doing what I'm doing right now, analyzing the dangers I see. I will continue searching for answers and getting the answers and more questions out, so the public will know about it, so at least we'll be ready when the time comes.

What I mean by "when the time comes" is when there will be

a major push to get our country under total control. That's the objective, the bottom line to these endless, mindless conflicts.

The "means of destruction" are the many insane conflicts popping up, with so many other chronic ones going on. Add to that the overboiling pot of nitroglycerin that is the tens of millions of people displaced and unable to provide even food and shelter for themselves. The net result is that the United States, the policeman of the world by default, can't keep up with stamping out the raging fires.

And that's the plan: to weaken the one nation with the power and determination to keep its people safe and maintain world peace—the United States.

Weaken it for what reason? For control, of course. So that One World Government, which has been in the making for an eon, can take control of the food and money that makes the world turn. But first they need to create a leader who would be universally accepted.

Who would we follow as our world leader? A savior, of course. Someone we are told will get us out of the spinning downward spiral we would be sent into.

The Man on the White Horse, naturally.

As I've said, there is control, manipulation, and premeditation involved in the worldwide epidemic of violence.

It's happening in a fashion not unlike what was described in the Revelation to John.

The Man on the White Horse is the Antichrist.

Here's the interesting thing: If what has been prophesied by others and me is correct, if biblical sources and the Book of Revelation are correct, then we are going through major changes. But the strangest thing of all is that there will be an Antichrist, some individual who basically takes the part of Satan and comes to this planet—or who may already be here—a person who people will just beg to protect and save us but who turns out to be the Antichrist, the villain of villains, who tries to destroy all life.

If you read the Book of Revelation, eventually life is good at the end, things work out for all of us, but it takes a thousand years. I'm very curious to see who that person might be. Is that person here already? It's anybody's guess. I've heard some outrageous things about who it might be. But I don't think they are who they say they are.

9

We must love one another or die.
—W. H. Auden, "September 1, 1939"

I also believe that, as part of this process where we find ourselves hurtling down an unmarked path full of dangerous curves that lack warning signs, we as a species are going through some incredible changes. I'm talking about our minds and souls, not our bodies.

As with other maladies affecting people and nations, the severe changes we have been going through are created by the interconnectedness that gives those who want control a way to exercise it.

I have felt, for the past several years now, that people are changing, that they're more uptight. You can see it in people both as a whole and individually. Road rage is not just frequent, it is a pandemic of anger and lashing out. Not infrequently, that lashing out results in the loss of life and in prison cells.

Yet, despite all the publicity—and the arrest of those involved—the rage is out there, on our streets, still happening.

An even crazier lashing out than road rage, if that's possible, are the enormous number of people, most commonly men, who are disappointed with their lives—usually their relationship or job—and act out their disappointment, their own failures, with rage toward innocent people, grabbing a gun and killing others before very commonly taking their own lives or committing "suicide by cop."

People often don't have any ability to just calm down—they're abrupt, they are rude to each other, and very soon it escalates into something vile and deadly.

Some of this is easy to understand. There are probably twice as many people on the planet today as there were when most middle-aged people were born. Sheer numbers alone mean there will be more competition, more rubbing of shoulders, more stress and aggravation as so much more of life becomes hurry up and wait, whether you're in bumper-to-bumper traffic on a freeway, in the checkout line at the supermarket, or even waiting to download something from the Internet.

The world is coming at us faster, too. News events flash around the globe, making "hits" on the digital devices—TVs, phones, computers, tablets—of hundreds of millions of people. Not just reported moments after an event has happened, but even taking us right to the event to see how it progresses—and climaxes.

We get live action of a tornado as it sweeps toward a school, coming closer and closer, until we see bits of roofing and then slabs of it and finally the whole roof ripped up and thrown to the wind. Turn to another channel and there may be someone on the edge of a tall building, ready to jump, while we stare, fixated on the suffering and agony of someone who believes that killing themselves is an escape from what is intolerable to them.

Many of us are unable to keep up the pace.

People are at a point where trust, family values, empathy, and even common sense have withered away.

Wherever I go, whenever I speak—and I do a number of these events all around the country—I feel an emptiness in people, people wishing to connect with people of like minds, people who truly want to reach out and become part of a bigger picture. And they're striving for this. It's a quest. Many of them can't find it, but they continue looking.

Mindless, endless wars and terror threats that seem to pop up here when it's been stamped out there, strange events and alienation, youth losing interpersonal skills because of the impersonality of electronic media, and wealth inequality all create a feeling of emptiness in people as they lose a little traction with their lives.

There's an interesting assessment of humanity in the movie *Contact* (1997), when the extraterrestrial is talking to Ellie, the Jodie Foster character, who is a SETI scientist searching for life in the universe. The alien says, "You're an interesting species. An interesting mix. You're capable of such beautiful dreams, and such horrible nightmares. You feel so lost, so cut off, so alone, only you're not. See, in all our searching, the only thing we've found that makes the emptiness bearable is each other."

I think that says it all. I think people are just looking to be with people that they like and enjoy, whether on this planet or on another one.

Many of us feel disconnected from what is going on around us because so much has changed so fast over the past couple of decades—changes that are often perplexing. It has left many of us with a feeling of emptiness.

We as a people need to get that back together, as humans stuck together on this big rock revolving around an aging sun.

I don't know how that's going to happen, because before it does we're going to go through tension, more strife, more police state actions.

People are struggling to find this continuity between each other, but it's going to take a while before they find that, and the gap in between is going to be a very difficult time for a lot of people.

There's something going on here, something is afoot. I can't quite put my finger on it, but I think people are sensing some kind of impending doom and it's affecting their psyches. These thoughts of doom are placed there by the same manipulation that is creating armies from the Dark Ages.

The change in society is prominently displayed by many young people, who have come into a world with different opportunities than what was presented to their parents and grandparents.

YOUNG PEOPLE ARE LOSING THE ABILITY
TO READ EMOTIONS

People send many vital nonverbal cues about the state of their emotions, their motives, and their actions. From face-to-face contact, we learn what body language such as eye contact, foot and finger tapping, fidgeting, etc. are signaling.

A 2014 UCLA study, described by Stuart Wolpert on the UCLA Newsroom Web site, noted that, for thousands of years, most social communication and social learning took place face-to-face, but that young people under eighteen today spend an average of nearly eight hours a day using mobile media and the Internet. Text messaging alone occupies more of teenagers' time than face-to-face communications.

The study found that as little as five days away from media screens significantly improved the ability of the pre-teen group studied to read nonverbal emotional cues such as facial expressions.

10

George Bernard Shaw said that youth is wasted on the young. But I wonder what he would have said if he knew that, today, young people have fewer opportunities to be financially independent than their parents and grandparents had at the same age. Those born in the electronic age, for the most part, find themselves in a world in which opportunities for higher education, careers, and home ownership are not as available as they were for their parents and grandparents.

As colleges and universities became moneymaking institutions instead of just citadels of higher education, the cost of a degree has skyrocketed, putting a major burden not only on the young but also on their parents. Incredibly, in some years, having a college degree has often hindered rather than enhanced the ability to find work.

In addition, the electronic age has victimized young people and caused many of them to be alienated from society. The young often fail to develop the ability to deal with people and situations as effectively as past generations because those born over the past couple of decades are living in a society where social media takes the place of one-to-one interaction.

I believe it will be an even more difficult time for young people than for those of us who have had many years of experience keeping our balance as world events shift the earth beneath our feet.

Although all of us have to deal with keeping our sanity as so many insane things happen in our world, we need to be aware that this digital age is taking a strange hold on our young people.

Phones and tablets, e-mails and texting, tweets and photo sharing, and all the other wonderful, marvelous gadgets that young
people experience are changing the way they think and behave.

The good part of this is that it helps keep young and old
connected with friends and family through social media, that
the young experience so many of the marvels of the world at an
early age and can access so much of the almost illimitable sources
of knowledge.

So much for the good part. Now let's talk about the bad
stuff—and I'm not just referring to the fact that you actually see
young *and* old sitting around a table with their heads in their
phones rather than relating with their companions.

The truly bad stuff is the neurobiological effect growing up
in the electronic age, the "digital revolution," has and is having
on young people, whose brains and social skills are being affected
in ways that may become irreversible.

I mentioned this in my novel *Night Talk*, and I bring up again
because it is such an important issue.

With so much knowledge and information, so many social
media "friends" at their fingertips, products of this digital age are
in many ways far more advanced than their parents and grandparents. But while they are able to surge ahead of their elders
in some ways, in other ways they have lost some fundamental
skills.

Human communication skills aren't just a good grasp of
language. Much of our communication is nonverbal—we tell
people many things, from pleasure to anger, by our body language. Subtle things like the way we make eye contact or the
stiffness of our posture can give us clues to how we are coming
across to the person we are communicating with. During a
job interview or while making a sales pitch, reactions as subtle
as fidgeting and foot tapping can be signals. These are not clues
that people can pick up by watching the other person on a screen,
whether it's a cell phone or a computer screen.

Being smart about what others think of you, being able to impress an employer in order to get a job, to deal with a customer to make a sale, or to understand the nuanced signals given by coworkers are difficult to learn watching a screen.

What is sad, disturbing, and even dangerous is that digital relationships are not completely honest, because they are easier to establish and are less demanding to maintain than ones that require face-to-face interaction. You don't get the whole person when you are viewing them on a screen a couple inches wide. And you won't recognize the dangers the person on the screen can present, because you are not seeing an image of a whole person.

Digital relationships can be turned off with the press of a button. That doesn't prepare young people for a world where there's no button that solves our problems.

The interconnectivity of everything, from relating to friends and family to our work and leisure time, created by the digital revolution, also creates a danger to our liberty.

By wiring us all together globally, are we being made to dance like puppets?

Is this interconnectivity part of the world control that is happening?

My answer to that is simple: Yes!

THE WEALTH GAP IS DEEPER THAN
THE GRAND CANYON

In a study of 16 countries, Americans had the greatest disconnect on the income gap, believing that top executives make about 30 times more than average workers. Execs actually make about 350 times as much.

You have no idea just how much more your boss' boss' boss is making compared to you.

—Elizabeth G. Olson, "Americans Have No Clue
Just How Much More CEOs Make,"
Fortune (October 13, 2014)

11

There is an ever-widening gap between those who possess insane amounts of wealth and those who have worked hard all their lives and see their assets shrinking every year.

As with so many other wrong turns our society is taking, the wealth gap is not an accident but a way of getting control over people.

I am not against a person possessing great wealth. I do not resent baby-faced billionaires who made their fortunes by coming up with some clever social media gimmick.

But when the wealth disparity between the rich and poor becomes akin to what it was in the days of kings with absolute power and their lazy nobles, I have to question whether it is reasonable. And I don't find it reasonable when the top one percent holds as much wealth as the bottom 90 percent—especially when about two-thirds of those possessing great wealth started with . . . yes, you guessed it, they started with great wealth, either inheriting it or marrying it.

I also dislike and distrust the insane gap between what CEOs earn, even with bad track records, compared to what hard-working people at lower levels take home. American CEOs are the highest paid in the world, with median compensation of $10.5 million in 2013. The median wage for workers was less than $27,000.

The compensation paid to CEOs has soared over the past decades. In the 1960s, it was thirty times the average worker's salary. In the 1990s, the gap increased to the point that CEO salaries were a hundred times that of the average worker.

Today, without increased productivity by CEOs as compared to workers to justify an ever-widening gap, CEOs earn about 350 times what an average worker does.

Some of these monster salaries are for CEOs leading companies that are going out backwards and taking the pension plans of workers as they go down. All while members of the board of directors sit on their hands.

There is also a wide racial wealth gap.

This incredible disparity is a tinderbox for society because it is creating a world where the differences between the haves and the have-nots, between those who shoulder the workload and the rich parasites who feed off of those who work the hardest, has become a dangerous perversion of what a fair and equitable society should be.

This ever-widening schism between the superrich and the people who work to keep the world running smoothly and orderly has created players on this planet who are so wealthy and so powerful that the game, for them, is control and manipulation.

A few hundred megarich donors to political parties are blocking tax reform that would cause them to lose the loopholes that keep them taxed at middle-class rates.

The situation is similar to the tax situation in France that led to the French Revolution. The infamous tax called the *taille* was a tax that each common household paid, while the nobility and the rich paid almost nothing. The wealth gap ultimately shattered the French economy and impoverished hardworking people.

The majority of these immensely wealthy controllers did not earn their stripes and their fortunes through hard work and innovation in tough industries but are of a moneyed class that inherited vast wealth and position but lacks the talent of those who actually earned the money.

As I'm writing this, I get this rather facetious image of Marie Antoinette wondering why hungry people don't eat cake.

The superrich count their money in billions, live in homes costing tens of millions of dollars, and use their wealth to make presidents and other world leaders. This, while a large portion of a generation of working-age young people still lives with their parents because they can't find a decent-paying job. These young people are often buried under enormous loans for schooling that hasn't opened the doors to employment for them.

This dichotomy is untenable, because society can't keep beating down people, holding them down, and often keeping them worse off than their parents—and their parents worse off than the generation before them.

At the same time, young people are more of a burden on their parents, who themselves are struggling to keep their own heads above water as whole industries are downsizing not their *profits*, which are pocketed by the elite one percent, but their *American workforce*, as they send jobs overseas and replace workers with machines. Factories and offices operated completely by robots are just around the corner.

This vast gap between what hardworking people still in the labor market earn, what retirees who worked decades for their pensions possess, and what the few financial elite earn cannot be sustained, because it is eroding the very basis of the foundation of what makes America a great and powerful country—the productive middle class that makes our offices and factories hum.

I often hear people speak about how different the world is today than the one they were born into. But the history of America has seen continuous growth, in which each generation is pretty much better off than the previous one . . . until this relatively recent, incredible financial schism between the superrich and the middle class.

We can't maintain an equitable society when there are so many people who do nothing to contribute to the common good or even earn their keep yet are doing grossly better than those who work hard to earn their daily bread and keep a roof over their heads.

That gap will continue to get wider and wider and wider. And, at some point, the have-nots will say, *I'm fed up. I'm not going to take it anymore.* It's happening now. We're seeing it happen in places where there's unrest. It's not just that people are concerned about the police and what policemen may be doing to people; it's the difference between the haves and the have-nots. We've seen videos of people looting stores, taking diapers and things, because they want what they don't have. And that's going to get worse. That's my prediction.

The superrich will protect themselves. They will band together with the forces that manipulate kings and politicians to ensure that their wealth and privileges are not disturbed. And that silent hand taking control will be strengthened by what they put into the coffers.

One of the reasons for the destruction of the middle class while the rich get richer is how taxes are assessed. The top four hundred income makers earn an average of a little over $260 million a year. That's five million dollars a week. That is a million dollars a day for a five-day workweek. These receivers of incredible income were taxed at just about the same rate as a single taxpayer earning eighty thousand dollars a year.

Although I don't want to discourage anyone from getting as much money as they can, whether it is earned or inherited, I find it bizarre that our tax laws do not tax individuals proportionately.

SHOW ME THE MONEY!

It looks like the Securities and Exchange Commission listened to Cuba Gooding Jr. when he told Tom Cruise to "Show me the money" in the movie *Jerry Maguire*.

In 2015, the SEC changed a long-standing rule that required CEO pay be released only in annual reports. The change requires that the pay be released to the public at large.

While the average CEO makes several hundred times the average employee, some of them are making *thousands* of times more money.

Which, by the way, isn't a bad thing if the CEO is worth it. Too often, the pay isn't based on what they bring to the company but on how many of their pals are on the board of directors. Or how lazy the board members are when it comes to policing executive pay.

PART II

HIGHER SENSE PERCEPTION

Some people have a higher sense perception that gives them the ability to glimpse what others can't see. Even peeks into the future.

12

Are there people who have a higher sense of perception about the world around them and what will happen in the future?

Prophets and seers with the ability to sense something of the future have appeared in historical accounts and religious texts for centuries. Among the accounts that seem to point to the ability of some to predict future events more accurately than the average person are, of course, accounts of charlatans whose only ability is to be exceptional liars.

In the modern age, the most famous and challenging was Edgar Cayce, who passed away in 1945.

Cayce was born in Kentucky in 1877. He was an unusual youth who spent time daydreaming or using his imagination. He preferred the company of grown-ups rather than other children, so much so that some people called him "Old Man" rather than his real name.

His grandfather died when Cayce was very young, and he began to have "visits" from his grandfather's spirit.

He was especially close to his grandmother, who died when he was sixteen. Before she passed, she told him that he was different from other youths in "strange ways" but that he should never be ashamed about being different.

The first recognition that he had a unique ability involved his own health, in his early twenties. He had been suffering from constriction of his ability to speak. He sought medical advice and was basically told that he would never speak in any more than a painful whisper.

When traditional medical advice didn't cure the problem, he

went into a self-imposed deep sleep, at the suggestion of a friend, and diagnosed his own medical condition while he was under. His diagnosis—that he had developed a chronic condition that hindered blood getting to his throat muscles—led to a cure.

He went on to analyze the conditions of others, giving thousands of diagnoses, with an incredible rate of success.

His usual method was to lie down and enter into a sleep state. The person requesting the diagnosis was usually not present and might in fact be thousands of miles away and in contact only by telephone. He would give a diagnosis while in the trance. When he awoke, he could not remember what he had said while in the trance.

Cayce believed that the unconscious mind has access to information that the conscious mind does not have. That theory might have been derided by many at the time, but today it not only is generally accepted that our minds continue to process information during our sleep but also anyone, like myself, who has woken from a deep sleep with an intuitive perception or insight into something recognizes both the power of the unconscious mind and the fact that it is capable of processing information we didn't even recognize we had while we were awake.

Called the "Sleeping Prophet" and the father of holistic medicine, Cayce became world famous. Among his clients were President Woodrow Wilson, Irving Berlin, George Gershwin, and inventor/businessman Thomas Edison.

Despite a vast number of real-life incidences in which Edgar Cayce was proven right in his remote viewing, most academics in the field of psychology reject the existence of extrasensory perception (ESP) because it has not been verified by university researchers. When a researcher does come up with results that support the existence of ESP, the research is attacked as faulty.

I do not believe that enough serious research has been done

in the field to reject the existence of ESP. Nor am I impressed by the type of research that has so often been done.

The research, which is almost always done in a university, typically involves testing the knowledge of college students or other volunteers about things beyond their five senses. The participants are usually "ordinary people" with no claims to possessing any knowledge beyond the five senses, or occasionally a celebrity type is invited in to test claims about their talent for extrasensory perception.

The participants are given tests that are intended to show whether they have ESP. An example of testing is to show the participant one side of a card and ask them to identify what is on the other side of it. This might be a number, a picture, a set of lines or other figures, or just about anything. The cards are sometimes called Zener or ESP cards. The person holding the cards can see what is on the cards but only shows the blank side to the person being tested.

In order to know what is on the card, the person being tested has to either read the mind of the person holding the card (since the person holding it knows what is on the card) or otherwise "sense" what is on the card. The third option is that the person simply makes a wild guess.

The basic idea is to get beyond guesswork and see whether any participant can consistently beat the odds, thus demonstrating that they have knowledge rather than just lucky guesses.

There are more ways to go at this, but a basic method is to test a bunch of people and see what happens.

Overall, despite some claims that a participant has gone beyond guessing, the results have been negative in these academic tests. And I can understand why, if the testing is done with a limited group of people: *There are more than seven billion people on the planet.* How many of those people would have to be tested before confirming that someone has ESP?

If there are seven Edgar Cayces in the world who can use extrasensory perception to diagnose medical maladies, you would have to test billions of people to find them. That doesn't mean that they don't exist, but it does mean that they are few and far between, making finding them pretty much impossible, unless they come forward and volunteer.

If you are testing people for a gift of prophecy, finding them in a university setting would be just as impossible, because not only would they, too, be few and far between but also their visions of the future would take years to validate.

One form of "beating the odds" is really quite incredible. There are people who have won a lottery multiple times. The odds of winning a state lottery can easily be one in tens of millions. The odds of winning a multiple-state lottery can get into one in hundreds of millions.

The odds are great, but somebody wins.

But what are the odds of winning a lottery multiple times when the winner has chosen numbers (as opposed to playing scratch tickets)? The chance must be infinitesimal. Yet people have won lotteries not just twice but many times. Is that an example of ESP at work? I don't know the answer to that.

I also don't know how many Edgar Cayces there are in this world who are able to remote view medical conditions, but I don't reject the existence of ESP on the grounds of what I don't know.

13

Hundreds of books and articles have been written about Edgar Cayce, his techniques, and his abilities.

One of the people who studied Cayce's work was my aunt, who was a very distinguished authority in the field of psychiatry, the late neuropsychiatrist Dr. Shafica Karagulla.

I call Dr. Karagulla my aunt, but she was actually my father's cousin.

Dr. Karagulla was a well-known, esteemed, and successful neuropsychiatrist. A medical doctor, she trained for psychiatry at the Royal Edinburgh Hospital for Mental and Nervous Disorders and later received fellowships in the areas of neurology and neurosurgery.

She became a member of the Royal College of Physicians of Edinburgh, the highest medical qualification in Britain, and then an assistant professor at the State University of New York. Ultimately, she became a U.S. citizen and a noted practicing physician.

When I knew her, she was a Los Angeles–based neuropsychiatrist who had become fascinated with brain states and consciousness after her case studies brought about conclusions that extended the foundations of contemporary knowledge of human awareness. She wrote a number of works on the subject, including the classic book that is literally a seminal treatise on many areas of the supernatural, *Breakthrough to Creativity*.

In the book, Dr. Karagulla describes how people can access higher states of awareness. She had the courage to study and report her findings on subjects that few psychiatrists, much less a person as distinguished as she was in her field, would even comment upon. These subjects included clairvoyance, telepathy, and out-of-body experience, most often relying upon actual case studies. Dr. Karagulla pointed out that the human brain has areas that are not functioning but are still evolving and could be used in future stages of development.

Even though she was a conventionally trained medical doctor, she was intrigued about the awareness of some people about knowledge or information that did not come from prior experience and that was not gained by the person's five senses. She asked whether humans were breaking through the five senses and developing what she called a higher sense perception.

Her interest was stimulated when a friend sent her a book about Edgar Cayce. This was more than a decade after his death. He had left behind a large quantity of information documenting his abilities, including thousands of recorded sessions in which he went into a trance and gave a diagnosis or other information. The friend also asked her to read Plato's allegory of the cave after she had learned about Cayce. In Plato's allegory, prisoners are chained so that, instead of seeing people and objects moving, they see shadows cast on the walls by puppeteers. Those shadows constitute truth and reality to the prisoners.

Dr. Karagulla found that Cayce's remarkable and well-documented abilities fell outside the knowledge she had gained through study, research, and the practice of neuropsychiatry. In plain English, it blew her mind, because there were no answers in traditional science to explain the phenomenon.

Reading Plato's allegory, she came to ask herself whether she wasn't one of those prisoners chained to one point of view, and she realized that she had to be open-minded about the ability of people to have higher sense perception.

Deciding that it was time a qualified scientist researched higher sense perception, she began a study and was surprised to find how many people had the ability—and that the number of people with a "breakthrough" in human consciousness was increasing.

14

I believe that I have an ability to look into the future. This is not conjecture or ego on my part. There have been times when I have been way ahead of myself in terms of some business concepts that never materialized—until twenty years later, when they popped and became big projects.

I don't claim to be psychic, but I do have an intense intuition.

I don't know how this happened. I was probably just born with it, and I've been able to use it for a lot of things in my own life. So when I anticipate things about the future, I go into my little meditative state, I go into my dream state, I think about these things, and I get these answers. I've been very intuitive to use it on *Coast to Coast*.

I think it helped me get the job on *Coast to Coast*. I would concentrate on the individuals who were responsible for hiring and, sure enough, they contacted me and things just worked out.

There's something in the universe that I call the wireless internet, which we're all connected to, and I somehow have been able to get on that wireless internet with a router that I have in my head and I'm able to do and go to a lot of places.

What I have described up to now, in terms of the path the world is taking—the deliberate path being set out for us—is partly from knowledge gained and partly from what I am seeing.

Here are some of my thoughts about what will happen in the world over the next few years.

Wealth inequality is as severe as it was during the days of absolute kings and nobility living in unimaginable luxury while the poor "ate cake." The gap between the very rich and the hardworking middle class will be aggravated by a major economic downturn that will hurt many people. This will lead to disruption both globally and in the corner of the world we occupy.

Wars and terrorism have been popping up on every continent, creating havoc, destroying fragile governments, making millions homeless and starving.

I believe the chaos is drawing the great powers into a dangerous game that will bring about an even greater war than the regional conflicts that we have been accustomed to dealing with.

A billion people in the world are without clean water to quench their thirst, and soon there won't be sufficient water to grow enough food to feed them.

They say armies march on their stomachs. When you cut the lines of food and water, armies with plenty of bullets must throw down their loaded weapons and surrender. People, like armies, also march on their stomachs. The food and water in the third world is being cut off by conflicts and a diminishing amount of available water while tens of millions of people displaced by these conflicts are fighting for enough substance to survive.

We are affected anytime a significant part of the world is thrown into chaos, whether by nature or by war, because the turmoil comes back to our door.

We also are not immune to internal economic or domestic havoc, despite being the world's most powerful nation. A gaping hole in our internal security is our dependence on the national power grid that underlies literally our entire economic superstructure. As I will show later, the grid that brings electricity to our homes, offices, financial institutions, factories, and farms is extremely vulnerable to collapse because our political leaders are too inept to properly protect it.

The Internet of Things, which I call the Internet of Everything, which is bringing interconnection to every part of our lives, is also seriously vulnerable to collapse. When it goes, it will pretty much cause similar chaos in our lives.

What I am seeing is not just a vulnerability in physical things. People, too, are changing. They are becoming more short-tempered and more unable to control rages at the same time that they are become more intolerant. Many people are consumed by a sense of doom and emptiness.

I see a great shadow over many of the world's most critical problems and raging conflicts. A shadow cast by a force most people don't see or realize exists, even while it drives us toward interconnectivity in an effort to control us.

Who is doing these things? What is the dark hand creating and manipulating conflict and chaos? Some secret society? A twenty-first-century, digital-age Illuminati that pulls the strings that make presidents and kings jump? A goal of One World Government? One World Economics? One World Digital Interconnectivity linking every soul on the planet?

What is their objective with regard to the United States, the world's most powerful stabilizing entity? To destabilize? Demoralize? Weaken? Take control?

Will there be a charismatic "leader" to "save" us from ourselves and the terrors that give us nightmares?

My answer is yes to all of the above.

How are they going to do it?

Manipulate climate and the weather to create drought to stop food production—and starve much of the world so that we turn on one another?

Take control of water and stop the flow until there are wars over water for drinking and crops?

Use our interconnectivity to shut down the power grid and the Internet, shutting us down with it?

We'll take a look at these and other ways control and domination is being engineered.

PART III

STRANGER THAN FICTION

My novel, *Night Talk*, is a work of fiction, a suspense thriller, but one that deals with many of the electronic invasions of our privacy and the degradation of our society by the erosion of the one-on-one, face-to-face ethic that makes us great. Because some of the issues raised in the novel are mentioned in this book, I need to tell you a little about the character and background of the novel.

15

Night Talk features a late night talk show host who becomes entangled in murder and intrigue when a conspiracy theory takes life. Anyone who reads the novel and listens to my show will recognize that the views about the government's intrusion into our lives, held by the book's protagonist, Greg Nowell, are similar to mine.

Greg tackles controversial subjects, from angels to aliens and government agencies so deep in shadow and fog that the puppet strings they use to exercise control are invisible. His radio show is a world of the paranormal and paranoia, where claims of alien abductions, Bigfoot sightings, and a mysterious world government are the norm. His investigations have not convinced him that every claim of paranormal activity is genuine, but it has convinced him that many claims deserve to be investigated, that almost all are ignored, and that there is enough evidence supporting some claims that a pattern of proof has been established.

Other than his passion for the truth about things that often are unexplainable, he keeps his own experiences and beliefs personal. He is a very private person but feels compelled to reach out to others and is free with his feelings about the state of the world.

His show has many kinds of callers, some with fear and anxiety about the world they live in, some with information or observations they want to share, and some who just want to vent about an injustice. Many sense that they live in a world that is manipulated by unknown forces that operate in secret.

Greg lashes out against the invasions of privacy and the dilution of human rights brought about by putting everyone under a microscope. Why do government and business need to gather so much information about people? To identify everyone by their facial features and monitor their use of phones, e-mails, and social networking? To know what we eat or read, the movies we watch, the clothes we wear, whom we admire and whom we hate—even the sex toys we buy and with whom we use them?

Each of us is dissected in a thousand different ways so businesses can pinpoint exactly what our needs and desires are and dangle them before us. And all that information is available to the government (shades of *1984* and *Brave New World*).

An American living in a metro area is photographed more than *two hundred times a day* by closed-circuit television cameras, on streets, in stores, and where they work. Mannequins with camera eyes are being placed near store entrances to identify customers from national facial databases, so information about their buying habits can be made available to salespeople.

Greg's world explodes when government agents accuse him of having received ultrasecret files from a hacker intent on exposing a secret cabal with tentacles throughout the government. The hacker is killed and the evidence points to Greg, who goes on the run as he is entangled in murder and stalked by a demented assassin.

As his life spirals out of control, Greg realizes his paranoia is really a heightened awareness of strange machinations, and he seeks help from people who would best understand: callers to his show who don't trust the government, have gone "under the radar," or are angry and paranoid about the vast gathering of information and invasions of privacy by government agencies.

Of course, it is no accident that the issues Greg Nowell tackles in *Night Talk* have similarities to the real-life ones I am tackling in the book you hold in your hand.

Although the intrigues surrounding Greg in *Night Talk* are fictional, as you read about the real-life conspiracies I am about to lay out for you, the conclusion you will come to is that truth is stranger than fiction.

Defeat? No, you don't understand because you really don't know people. Having a college degree that says you do doesn't count. Ethan started something, set a wave of information into motion that will keep moving, slowly, just a little at a time, but someday it will be a tsunami that will rip apart all the facades that creatures and traitors like you have been hiding under. You're a traitor, a quisling, and you'll end up as all turncoats do.

—Greg Nowell, in George Noory's
Night Talk (2016)

PART IV

WHAT WE IGNORE CAN KILL US

We will deal with some major issues critical to our health, welfare, and even survival as a nation and world power, matters that also have immense personal impacts on each of us and on our families and yet are being ignored by our political leaders.

The issues facing us are national and global ticking bombs with a potential for incredible devastation and catastrophic consequences.

We will start with a threat that I have been working for some time, trying to create public awareness and educate our political leaders.

It is a disaster waiting to happen and it has to be dealt with now, because studies by top scientists say that it has happened before and will happen again in the near future.

It's the Big One that will be coming at us.

16

THE BIG ONE COMING AT US

If an asteroid big enough to knock modern civilization back to the 18th century appeared out of deep space and buzzed the Earth-Moon system, the near-miss would be instant worldwide headline news.

Two years ago [2012], Earth experienced a close shave just as perilous, but most newspapers didn't mention it. The "impactor" was an extreme solar storm, the most powerful in as much as 150+ years.

"If it had hit, we would still be picking up the pieces," says Daniel Baker of the University of Colorado.

—Tony Phillips, "Near Miss: The Solar Superstorm of July 2012," *NASA Science* (July 23, 2014)

Those comments from a NASA publication introduce our next subject, an incredible danger to our entire civilization, which I have been working to wake up our nation about: solar storms, fiery eruptions that shoot off the sun and carry incredible potential for disaster through damage to the electric power grid that provides us with most of what makes our homes, TV and communications, farms, and factories run.

These violent solar eruptions that shoot out to Earth are called by different names (solar storms, solar flares, solar EMPs, the Carrington Event), but regardless of the name, the potential result is pretty much the same: the sun can lash out and fry electrical systems worldwide.

The "flare" is what roars out from the sun's surface and hurtles at us. In its wake is a tornado of destructive electromagnetic energy. When it hits Earth, it creates an electromagnetic pulse (EMP) that can be damaging to anything electrical—which is just about everything in our high-technology civilization.

For the sake of simplicity, I refer to the entire phenomenon, from solar storm to the damage it causes, as a "flare," rather than getting technical.

We had a near miss from a flare in 2012, which we will discuss. A study indicates we have a *12 percent* chance of getting hit by one by 2024. That's about a one in eight chance of what could be an earth-shattering event. That's high odds, as far as I'm concerned.

We will examine how these devastating flares occur, and I will explain other potential threats to the highly vulnerable power grid that could put us back a hundred years, including a cybercrime or terrorist attack on the power grid, which can knock out power for tens of millions, or a nuclear EMP created by an aerial nuclear explosion.

Before we get into the havoc that would be created in our daily lives by a devastating flare from the sun or an attack by hackers or terrorists, I will lay out for you what the power grid is and why it is so vulnerable.

17

Most of us are familiar with the term "power grid." In broad terms, it's the network that delivers electricity from generating sources to the entities and individuals that consume it nationwide. Although it is interconnected, it's composed of many different companies and facilities, ranging from plants that produce electrical power to substations and towers and lines traversing the nation to distribute that power.

Power plants generate electricity by burning coal, gas, or oil, by harnessing atomic energy, or hydroelectrically. The plants send extremely high-voltage electricity on lines carried by tall steel transmission towers. From this starting point, the high-voltage electricity travels to more towers to feed substations, getting "stepped down" from extreme high voltage along the way, until it is fed into electrical panels at homes and businesses.

Often the towers, poles, and lines are not set out in neat rows but are gathered together in a metal forest, a mesh of frames, cables, wires, and big steel boxes containing mysterious things like transformers, regulator banks, feeders, and other electrical equipment.

Pretty simple and basic . . . right?

Wrong. Because the word picture I just drew leaves out the most important aspect of today's power grid: the fact that it can go down like dominos in a row.

I described power grids as if each was a self-contained unit, from making power to delivering it to users. That was true in the early days, when power grids were first built, but as the country grew and the demand for electricity soared everywhere, the grid here got connected to the grid there and pretty soon it was one big national and international interconnected system.

When interconnection occurred, what happened in Vegas no longer stayed in Vegas. Instead it affects Iowa City, New York, Los Angeles, Boston, and just about everywhere else in the country. The interconnectedness permits power to be transmitted and used most efficiently. A surplus in Michigan, near the Canadian border, could be directed down to New Orleans, on the Gulf of Mexico, if needed.

So when I use the expression "power grid," I'm not referring to the local or even the regional network but to the whole vast, interdependent system that feeds power to hundreds of millions of people in North America alone. Quite a vast monstrosity, considering that the original power "grids" in the nineteenth century were small units built near or on-site at factories and businesses that used the electricity.

What is particularly astounding about the grid is that it looks fairly passive—unless there's a dam turning generators with thousands of gallons of water or we look inside a power plant where gas or oil is burned to turn turbines and generators to produce and transmit electricity.

We get the same impression if we look at the flow of electricity in our homes. The electrical current itself is quiet and invisible. It's not obvious—it's just there. It isn't something we think about unless we are paying the bill—or it goes out and we quickly realize how much it affects our daily lives.

But the grid is a silent monster. High-voltage lines can carry hundreds of thousands of volts each, and the billions of volts being carried over a vast area are incredibly sensitive in terms of precision—a tiny deviation in directing the massive flow of this powerful, even violent stuff can have widespread consequences.

The power grid is in fact a dangerously unwieldy system that will disrupt our lives unless basic flaws are corrected.

18

Put away whatever confidence you have in our electric companies and our elected officials at the local, state, and federal level in terms of making sure the power grid is secure. The truth is that it is not secure, and not only against attacks on it. In fact, it is so inherently vulnerable that it is capable of tripping over its own feet and crashing, as it has done in the past.

An example of what the power grid can do to itself, even without a solar flare or terrorist attack, started with what should have been a minor glitch and ended up shutting down the power for *fifty-five million people*. The most amazing thing about the blackout was how quickly and easily the vast system unraveled as plants went down like dominos over a wide area.

It was the afternoon of August 14, 2003, during a period of high usage, when overhead power lines came into contact with a tree south of Cleveland, Ohio. The break in the line caused an overload and shutdown in the plant serving the area. But the overload condition didn't stop there. That malfunction caused more lines and power generating plants to overload, one after the other, cascading, until about fifty-five million people, served by 265 generating plants in the Northeast, Midwest, and Ontario, Canada, were affected.

A reason no one put a brake on the system, and plant after plant went down like falling dominos, is that the local area grid's electronic alarm system suffered a "software glitch." Because the alarm did not work, grid operators were without notice that they needed to reduce or redistribute power, and business went on as usual, with facilities in other areas continuing to send high voltage over the lines.

In other words, a vast network of electric grids, serving tens of millions of people over a wide geographic area, crashed because a single local alarm was not triggered—and there was no backup system, no fail-safe device to stop a disaster from spreading when one system failed.

Among the many questions about how this could happen, one has to wonder why anyone who knew anything about computers wouldn't create a backup system to take over when a "software glitch" occurred. This was not a small business entity but a crisis in which the economic impact was in the billions. Even small business owners and consumers back up their systems.

It was the largest blackout in United States history and, at that time, was second in size only to a 1999 blackout in Brazil. The Brazilian blackout started when a lightning strike at an electricity substation started a chain reaction that affected nearly a hundred million people.

The 2003 blackout and the loss of electricity to homes and businesses caused widespread problems, ranging from loss of lights and train service to some water plants shutting down. The effect lasted a matter of a day in some areas and up to a week in more rural places.

The point I am making about the massive blackout is not about its long-term effect but about how vulnerable the power grid is to malfunctions. This massive assault on power for fifty-five million people spread over a large region came about from a tree limb hitting a power line. Brazil went down due to a lightning strike.

Now imagine what would happen if a solar flare struck with millions of times the radiation of a lightning strike—a solar flare like the near miss in 2012, which has a 12 percent chance of striking Earth by 2024.

This type of hit on the power grid, called a Carrington Event, would not put the grid out for hours or for days but for years, creating not just a blackout of our lights and the thawing of the food in our freezers but also, according to the NASA article, taking us back technologically to the eighteenth century.

That's more than two hundred years ago.

Remember the proverb about the how the lack of a horseshoe nail can result in a lost kingdom? The designers of a power grid that can be taken down by a tree limb should have heeded the words of Ben Franklin:

A little neglect may breed mischief: for want of a nail, the shoe was lost; for want of a shoe the horse was lost; and for want of a horse the rider was lost.

—Benjamin Franklin, *Poor Richard's Almanac* (1757)

19

We've seen what a tree limb and a lightning bolt can do to the power grid. Now we'll look at what a solar or man-made "flare" can do to the grid, and how frighteningly little is being done to prevent a disaster that can affect all of us personally.

I started this section with a NASA article that points out that our planet barely missed a global disaster that would have had catastrophic consequences, and that another such event is on the horizon. News of a major solar incident that has basically been ignored by the government and the public was a real wake-up call for me. After seeing that article, I got the message out loud and clear that something has to be done.

As I was to discover, when it comes to solar flares that could rip our nation and world apart, even less is being done than the little that is being done about those asteroids that whiz by us without warning or detection until it's too late.

"Do little or nothing" appears to be the plan to prevent earth-shattering disasters.

A really amazing aspect of the 2012 flare is that it pretty much got ignored by the press and the world at large. However, I did talk about the incident on *Coast to Coast*, and I started a campaign to educate the country about these events, in order to get our political and military leaders moving on protecting the system.

In addition to sharing my own feelings about the dangers of solar and man-made EMPs and the shocking lack of concern on the part of our politicians and military leaders, I invited experts on the danger to my show to speak to my audience, including F. Michael Maloof, a former security policy analyst in the Office of the Secretary of Defense, and William R. Forstchen, a professor of history at Montreat College in North Carolina and author of the informative novel *One Second After*.

The experts gave a great number of chilling facts and predictions about how vulnerable our power grid is to solar and man-made attacks.

Forstchen's *One Second After*, which deals with the consequences of a meltdown of our electrical system (in the book, it was an EMP caused by a nuclear explosion), lays out in great detail how our daily lives would be affected by an electrical storm. The storm from a nuclear EMP is similar to what would happen in the case of the solar storm predicted by 2024.

Let's take a step back and look at the solar storm that got me into action on a mission to educate the nation about potential consequences we can't ignore.

On July 23, 2012, a superstorm on the sun shot out a shock wave of solar energy. It came from a gigantic solar eruption and flew out from the sun as a solar flare, a torrent of energy and X-rays traveling at the speed of light, followed by a massive burst of electromagnetic radiation called a coronal mass ejection. A coronal mass ejection, in terms of "space weather," is akin to a gigantic tornado or hurricane traveling at more than five million miles per hour.

In this case, the violent superstorm of solar energy soared across Earth's orbit around the sun. But I am able to relate this story in calm detail because, when the powerful tempest crossed Earth's orbit, *it missed us.*

I will explain what would have happened if it had hit, and why the grid is a ticking bomb, ready to explode with the next powerful solar storm or even a terrorist attack, but first I want to give you some of the background about devastating storms from space, solar flares, and the like. You see, this isn't the first time we've been hit by an electromagnetic superstorm. And it won't be the last time.

The reason our planet is so sensitive to the sun's solar winds and storms is that we are surrounded by a magnetic field, also called the geomagnetic field. It extends pretty much from Earth's interior to where it meets the solar wind, a stream of charged particles spit out by the sun.

An electromagnetic storm can be thought of as analogous to a hurricane or tornado here on terra firma. What happens is that there are "storms" on the sun. From them, solar winds, solar flares, and even more violent coronal mass ejection tempests come shooting out from the sun, and they hit Earth when we get in the way.

These solar events bring shock waves of violent energy that disturb Earth's magnetic field, causing geomagnetic storms that can, among other things, cause strong currents in our power grids. Sudden powerful spikes in the storm can cause massive disruptions. If they are powerful enough, it would be like detonating a nuclear bomb high in the atmosphere to create a violent geomagnetic storm that guts our power grid.

It's difficult to trace the complete history of electromagnetic storms and EMPs back through the centuries because, other than causing incredible aurora borealis, or northern lights, its effect is on electricity. So we essentially have to stay within the historical time during which we've had widespread electricity.

The most powerful flare on scientific record is the Carrington Event of 1859.

The middle of the nineteenth century was not an era when electricity and lights were in general use. However, the telegraph, sometimes called the Victorian Internet, was in common use. The telegraph system was comprised of strings of wood poles and copper lines strung around the country, often following railroad tracks. In 1859, the commercial telegraph system was only about twenty years old and hadn't even reached the West Coast of the United States yet.

Awareness of the incident started when an amateur British astronomer, Richard Carrington, observed a solar flare. Following the flare, telegraph lines became highly electrified, operators received electric shocks, and telegraph lines and equipment were damaged.

The northern lights were so bright that they lit up areas as far south as Cuba and Hawaii. In the Rocky Mountain region and to the north, they glowed so brightly that people believed it was morning. All over the northern hemisphere, people gathered on streets and rooftops to watch the celestial light show.

But it wasn't a world-shattering event. The reason, of course, is that in 1859 there was very little electrical equipment to be affected by the solar superstorm.

In 1921, when electricity was in common use but the vast power grid was not yet fully interconnected, there was another powerful superstorm, though it is estimated that it was only about half as powerful as the one in 1859.

There have been other solar flare events, including the infamous 2012 event that missed us but that may pay another visit by 2024.

The remarks made by Dr. Vincent Peter Pry, a member of the congressional EMP Commission, are startling—and frightening. According to Pry, an EMP could result in the deaths of 90 percent of the people in the United States, due to starvation, disease, and the collapse of modern society. Moreover, the grid could be down for months or years, taking with it the critical infrastructure of modern society.

Let's take a closer look at the damage a natural or man-made EMP could do to us on a national and personal level, right down to our daily lives.

EMP ATTACK ON U.S. WOULD BE "CATASTROPHIC," CONGRESS TOLD

An Electromagnetic Pulse (EMP) attack on the United States, whether man-made or naturally occurring, could result in the deaths of nine out of ten Americans through starvation, disease and the collapse of modern society, warned Dr. Vincent Peter Pry, a member of the congressional EMP Commission and executive director of the Task Force on National and Homeland Security.

"A natural EMP catastrophe or nuclear EMP attack could blackout the national electric grid for months or years and collapse all the other critical infrastructures—communications, transportation, banking and finance, food and water—necessary to sustain modern society and the lives of 310 million Americans," Pry this week told the House Committee on Homeland Security Committee's Subcommittee on Cybersecurity, Infrastructure Protection, and Security Technologies.

—Amanda Vicinanzo, *Homeland Security Today*
(May 14, 2014)

20

I was a kid pre–Star Wars, growing up before its big box office receipts and merchandising rights made science fiction the stuff of blockbusters. In those days, sci-fi didn't set movie attendance records—few sci-fi movies were made, and the special effects were of the rubber band and Scotch tape variety. Fantastic stories were mostly the stuff of paperback novels that were so cheap they came two to a book and of pulp magazines that paid pennies a word to writers.

I remember a story from those days that I probably read in a pulp magazine, one of those imaginative tales about what happened to the world after a major global disaster caused by war or Mother Nature. "What happens after the Big One" was a pretty typical conversation piece for the generation that grew up during the nuclear saber rattling of the atomic age.

I don't recall what particular disaster caused the damage in the story; atmospheric atomic explosions or a scaring solar flare were the probable culprits. The electromagnetic effect of high-altitude nukes and solar eruptions can be pretty similar, so both worked to get across the end result: most everything in the world that was mechanical and had some sort of relationship to electricity stopped working—lights, televisions, cars, airplanes, you name it, none of them worked.

What stayed with me about the story was that it caused a reversal of socioeconomic status in society. Because the nukes or solar storms had created electromagnetic storms that fried everything electrical, and most things mechanical run off an electric element, simple hand tools became extremely valuable, while complex mechanisms were worthless.

The person who owned a hammer or a plumber's wrench was richer than people with fancy cars, yachts, and millions in the bank. After the blast, the cars and boats wouldn't run, the money couldn't be used to buy anything, but that hammer and wrench could fix a roof or a toilet.

I thought about the story after learning about that 2012 close call with a solar storm that could have created a global electromagnetic disaster.

I don't know how many times we've had close calls with global nuclear holocaust because of human error, human evil, or intercontinental missiles that have become rusty from decades of sitting around waiting to be used to destroy the world, but the history of hits and misses, and the mathematical probability of disasters, caused by EMPs makes me think about the world being in a position where wrenches are more valuable than yachts—for those of us who survive.

Rich or poor, famous or just average, the more you possess, the more you can lose if the grid is fried.

21

When I think about the things that would be affected by a flare, something akin to the fire and brimstone of the Revelation to John comes to mind.

How do you prepare for a scenario like that? I suppose the bottom line is not only to think about what you won't have after the grid goes down because it won't work but also to think about what you do have that will work even without electric power—the hammer-and-wrench scenario.

Let's start by looking around the house. The first thing to understand is that everything that feeds off your electric panel will not work after the grid goes down. That means all that direct wiring to lights, air-conditioning, heat, stoves, washers, and dryers won't work.

Gas stoves will not work for two reasons: they usually operate with an electric igniter, and even if you can light a burner with a match, the equipment that brings gas across the country to your doorstep won't be working.

Nor will the things we plug in work—that means no television, radio, wireless, Internet, or phones. Also no refrigerator, freezer, coffeemaker, or microwave.

So we are in a house without lights or the ability to cook. Depending on the weather, we may be freezing or sweating.

But we are not through yet. That water that comes out of the tap, that we drink, bathe in, and use to flush the toilet—it will be gone soon. Yes, water is also cleaned and pumped by equipment that relies on the grid.

What will work around the house? A charcoal or propane barbeque will be terrific until we run out of whatever fuels it. A fireplace is great if it runs off of wood and we live in a forest.

Most cars won't work because their ignition is electronic. Some older cars might still operate, but they won't be able to fill up because gas stations need electricity to operate.

You can't call 911, and even if you could get ahold of the police, coast guard, the army, or the navy, they—and millions of other local, state, and federal employees—are in the same boat you are. Nothing is working—their cars won't run; communications devices won't operate.

None of us can get to work unless we walk, and for the vast majority of us, there is nothing we can do at work. No lights, no phones, no elevators, no toilets, no . . . Nothing, really. Anything you have around that takes a battery will work—until the battery wears down and you need to buy new ones.

That money that you have saved for an emergency? Obviously, banks and ATMs won't work. The stock market is kaput. How valuable is money itself, if you had a hoard of cash?

At some point early on, people will come to the realization that money is pretty much worthless. That point is when it is a question of *survival*—we need food, water, and shelter as a minimum, even if we can make it without medical assistance.

Money—paper or bars of gold—can't be eaten or drunk, and at some point, you won't be able to buy anything to eat or drink.

People in major metropolitan areas will have it worse than people in smaller communities. Those in rural areas, especially if they have fireplaces and water wells, will do the best.

You can imagine how difficult it would be to get into a store that has no lights or registers working to try to buy a battery. The chances are that, by the time you got there, it would have already been looted of water, batteries, and nonperishable food by people as desperate as you are. Smart employees will stock up before the event begins.

Of course, once the stores are out of product, which could happen in *hours* due to panic, no more supplies would be coming in. Farmers won't be able to transport their goods to market. Food manufacturers can neither process nor transport their products. The stores will be empty after the employees and looters get through clearing the shelves.

Do I have to tell you that those of us in airplanes at the time the EMP hits most probably will be killed?

Medical assistance, hospitals, pharmacies, doctors, emergency personnel, the entire scope of most "modern" medicine, would be wiped away. No diagnostic testing, blood tests, or X-rays; no CT, MRI, or ultrasound scans; no kidney dialysis machines. Most hospital equipment, from oxygen to operations, relies upon electricity, not to mention the elevators, the toilets, and the drinking water.

Bandages, tourniquets, setting bones by feel would still be done.

I am not trying to be facetious, but the doctor who is good with a scalpel or has an ability to listen to a person's vital signs and diagnose illness will be infinitely more important than the medical scientist who builds machines that can cure millions but are useless after the grid goes down.

A study by the National Academy of Sciences estimated that a storm today like the one that heated up telegraph lines in 1859 would be a colossal catastrophe, with an impact in the trillions of dollars, and might take years to repair.

What countries in the world would fare the best following the impact of an EMP?

It should come as no surprise that the countries with the most complex and advanced technological superstructures would be hit the hardest. The United States, Europe, Japan, and major cities throughout the world, from New York to Rio to Hong Kong, would be in utter chaos and ruin in short order.

Third world countries, in general, would withstand the impact of a massive electromagnetic storm better than "richer" countries, because their superstructure is not as dependent upon high-tech electronics.

That doesn't mean it wouldn't devastate big cities everywhere. The people who are going to dodge the bullet best are those in rural areas. And if the rural areas are in third world regions like large sections of Africa, Asia, and the southern Americas, where toilets often don't work off a city sewer system and there are few household appliances and perhaps not even electricity, the effect will be the least.

Remember the story about the wrench and the yacht? Who do you think will be better off after a violent EMP knocks out grids globally—the billionaire in a Manhattan penthouse or the Peruvian farmer who lives in a shack and grows his or her own food?

I mentioned earlier that a fictional account of what would happen if the grid is fried can be found in William R. Forstchen's novel *One Second After*.

THE DAY THE SUN BROUGHT DARKNESS

On Friday March 10, 1989, astronomers witnessed a powerful explosion on the sun. Within minutes, tangled magnetic forces on the sun had released a billion-ton cloud of gas. It was like the energy of thousands of nuclear bombs exploding at the same time. The storm cloud rushed out from the sun, straight towards Earth, at a million miles an hour. . . .

March 12 the vast cloud of solar plasma (a gas of electrically charged particles) finally struck Earth's magnetic field. . . . It actually created electrical currents in the ground beneath much of North America. . . . In less than 2 minutes, the entire Quebec power grid lost power. . . .

Across the United States from coast to coast, over 200 power grid problems erupted within minutes of the start of the storm.

—Dr. Sten Odenwald, NASA.gov (March 13, 2009)

22

Hackers can bring down the grid.

Cybercrime is increasing at mind-boggling speed—and the power grid could be its biggest potential victim.

Once a rare event that captured our imagination, cyber-attacks have become common; even ones that make international headlines, and often have international consequences, have become old news to many people.

They should not be old news to anyone whose job it is to protect a computer network, because not only has the nature of hackers changed over the years but also the target of the attacks has changed, much to our potential detriment.

My image of those in the world of cyber-attacks used to be that of a young person with thick glasses and a wide-eyed, maniacal expression hacking into a corporate site in order to embarrass the company. The hacking was usually done for the same reasons some people climb mountains: the challenge.

My perception of the world of computer hacking changed when one of the seven deadly sins—greed—came into the picture. As the horror stories about identity theft rose and hackers started stealing the personal and credit card information of tens of millions of people in one fell swoop, I began to get concerned about how my personal information and that of my family are stored.

The concern about cybercrime took on more national and global consequences when big business got into the act of cyber spying.

Let's say a company in Shanghai wants a shortcut to cutting-edge technology developed for an aerospace firm in Seattle. Why bother buying it or hiring spies for industrial espionage, which could take years, when you can hire a hacker to invade electronically?

The worldwide consequences of hacking took on even more serious dimensions when nations themselves got into the act, kicking it up more notches than thrill seekers or credit card thieves can imagine.

One of the most famous incidents is the Stuxnet incident, in which the United States and Israel allegedly put malware into Iranian systems, targeting Iran's nuclear bomb building program. Malware is the generic term for intrusive software like computer viruses, worms, ransomware, and Trojan horses. Stuxnet was said to be the biggest and most expensive malware development known at the time.

The use of national attacks on another nation's computerized infrastructure can be a dangerous instrument, because nations can marshal more money and more tech workers than private industry and can potentially create attacks that could have consequences for millions of consumers. This goes beyond illegal purchases on credit cards or corporate bottom lines. These attacks can target the very infrastructure of a nation.

There are allegations thrown back and forth by one country or another that cyber spying and cyber sabotage is occurring. North Korea is usually high on the list of countries making allegations or being accused of using cyber programs as a weapon.

This all comes back around to the power grid and its vulnerability to attack. The power grid has to rank at the top of any hacker's list, whether the hacker is a thrill-seeking kid or an out-of-control rogue nation.

We have already talked about the terrible consequences that significant downtime of the power grid would have. One interesting study sets out the dollar value of the damage. Lloyd's, the insurance carrier, and the University of Cambridge Centre for Risk Studies did a study which revealed that if one hundred of the seven hundred Northeastern U.S. power generators went down, creating a blackout for a period of four days, the economic damage would be one trillion dollars. Keep in mind that a trillion is a thousand billion!

Terrorists can also bring down the grid.

Some years ago, a friend suggested to me that if a backpack or suitcase nuke was exploded on Wall Street by a terrorist, the financial consequences to the United States could turn our country into a third world economy.

That same assertion can be put forth if, instead of a nuclear weapon, the terrorist—or terrorist nation—infected the power grid with computer malware that caused a widespread blackout across the nation.

One immediate comparison between a nuclear bomb and computer malware is evident: you don't need hundreds of billions of dollars, a bunch of different factories, or decades of effort by thousands of highly qualified technicians and scientists, aided by blue-collar workers by the tens of thousands, to make computer malware.

I can't imagine why the geek who started hacking for the thrill of it at the age of fourteen and graduated to stealing credit card information would not have the technical know-how to accomplish something like that.

There are estimates that the Stuxnet malware, which was revealed in 2010, took somewhere between five and thirty people up to six months to prepare. Fine. Now that it's been done, how long would it take the geek to come up with not just an equal program but even one much more devastating, after all these years?

I believe the power grid is so important and so vulnerable

that I stay active in its defense and will continue to do so, even if the government finally moves to provide adequate protection. I have had experts such as Peter Pry, Michael Maloof, and William Forstchen on the show to discuss progress being made in securing the grid from catastrophic failure or destruction, and I will continue to be both a voice and an outlet for discussion of power grid issues.

The problem with dealing with matters of extreme national importance is that our political system has been broken so badly and for so long that it's difficult to get a governmental body or a legislator to do anything more complicated than decide what to have for lunch the next time out with a lobbyist.

U.S. POWER GRID VULNERABLE TO
CYBER ATTACKS

The U.S. power grid is a privileged target for various categories of attackers, terrorists, cyber criminals, and state-sponsored hackers. Daily, they threaten the backbone of the American society. Security experts and U.S. politicians are aware that the national power grid is vulnerable to a terrorist attack.

"It's possible; and whether it's likely to happen soon remains to be seen," explained the former Secretary of Defense William Cohen on *The Steve Malzberg Show.*

Attackers have several options to hit a power grid, from a cyber-attack on SCADA [supervisory control and data acquisition] systems to an EMP attack, according to Cohen.

"You can do it through cyber-attacks, and that's the real threat coming up as well. We have to look at cyber-attacks being able to shut down our power grid, which you have to remember is in the private sector's hands, not the government's. And we're vulnerable," Cohen added. "It's possible and whether it's likely to happen soon remains to be seen."

—Pierluigi Paganini, "Cyber Attacks on the Power Grid:
The Specter of Total Paralysis," InfoSec Institute
(July 27, 2015)

23

The mad scientist with an EMP death ray.

Who was this strange and brilliant genius with a connection to the power grid and EMPs, whose work led to the grid, death rays, and visits from extraterrestrials?

Nikola Tesla, of course, as I'm sure many readers had already guessed.

The power grid we utilize today came about because Tesla's invention of a practical way to supply alternating current revolutionized electrical power output, but he also actually came up with an electromagnetic pulse weapon.

Tesla was a Serbian-American inventor, scientist, engineer, genius, and eccentric. Able to speak eight languages, he is said to have been able to memorize complete books and to have an eidetic memory, capable of envisioning and reproducing visual images. He boasted that he kept most of his ideas in his head rather than putting them down on paper.

Even though his many patents earned him large sums of money, he spent so much money developing concepts that were, to say the least, overly ambitious, and he often teamed with men of finance, who took the lion's share of profits, that he possessed little at the time of his death. He never married and lived most of his time in America, nearly sixty years, in various hotels in the New York area.

He wrote in his autobiography that, over the years, he experienced blinding flashes of light that were accompanied by visions. Sometimes the visions provided the solution to a problem he was working on.

Despite modest means and a haphazard education, he rose to be a leading figure in the emerging field of electricity, often working with—and sometimes against—other giants of the era, Thomas Edison and George Westinghouse.

Tesla's relationship to the power grid is that he invented the alternating current (AC) that most of the world runs on today. Edison and Westinghouse were also involved, but it was Tesla who actually came up with the workable system. Westinghouse was an advocate of direct current (DC), and a technical and financial battle for the future of electricity took place that is called the War of Currents.

Essentially, direct current is what our lights and appliances work off of, but it was costly to distribute. Alternating current could be sent at a higher voltage and then stepped down for use. In general, alternating current was less expensive to transmit and distribute.

With Edison's financial help, Tesla won. And today, we have the vast network of power stations and lines carrying high voltage that is stepped down to usable voltage by the time it reaches our doorsteps.

One of Tesla's dreams, in which he was decades ahead of the world, was wireless transmission of electric power and communications—the stuff of our cell phones, laptops, TV, radio, the Internet, and many other products. He built a boat that was controlled wirelessly.

He had the incredible idea of harnessing the very power of the electromagnetic forces of Mother Earth to send electricity wirelessly rather than along copper wires strung between poles. He died without accomplishing that vision.

What he does claim to have accomplished was communications with extraterrestrials and a death ray weapon. In 1899, he said, he received communications from another planet in our solar system, what he called "intelligently controlled signals." He also claimed to have worked for decades on a mysterious weapon that others called a death ray. Somewhat similar to a solar flare, the ray gun would direct concentrated beams of particles at enemy aircraft and armies. Although he claimed to have developed the weapon, which he believed was so powerful it could end all war, he died without revealing it.

The best thing I can say about this incredible human being is that, when you compare him to the titans of the computer, they don't make 'em like they used to.

Nikola Tesla was one of a kind.

24

A death ray for killer asteroids?

It's too bad we don't have Tesla's death ray to take care of a danger from the sky that even exceeds EMPs in potential danger.

"Near-Earth objects" is what they are called. That's kind of a milquetoast label for an object the size of a house that can destroy cities and kill millions, or bigger ones, a few miles wide, that can destroy human and animal life on our planet by creating so much ashy dust in the sky that the sun gets blocked out and nothing grows—as the dinosaurs found out.

We earthlings have been incredibly lucky and have dodged the killer asteroid doomsday scenario, but there have been close calls for widespread damage. In 2013, a near-Earth object (i.e., killer asteroid) the size of a two-story house blew up in the atmosphere near a Russian city, injuring more than 1,500 people with flying debris and glass. Fortunately, it didn't directly hit the city, which has a population of more than a million people, because it exploded with the power of thirty thousand Hiroshima bombs. Had it hit the city itself, the loss of life would have been staggering.

Russia's Siberia, of course, was the scene of another huge aerial explosion, the Tunguska event in 1908, which knocked down an estimated eighty million trees over an area of nearly a thousand square miles. Had it hit a city, the consequences are, again, too terrible for words.

Tactics to prevent the unimaginable consequences of a direct hit include an early warning system, so people can be evacuated, and a weapon to destroy or divert the asteroid. Nudging the asteroid out of its rendezvous with our planet, by the way, is considered the best bet, because blowing it up could create a large number of smaller pieces that would come flying down.

Of course, we don't have an early warning system. On the contrary, asteroids that could cause considerable damage periodically whiz by, often with only hours of warning. And we don't have a delivery system for a weapon.

NASA knows what is needed, but it doesn't get enough funding, fast enough, to do what is needed—more satellites and telescopes scanning the sky for small objects, and putting in place a system to avoid catastrophe when something comes streaking at us at high speed.

There are an estimated million near-Earth objects in our solar system. We have cataloged only a small fraction of them.

We'd better get busy and start increasing our knowledge about what else—and who else—is occupying some of the "space" our planet flies in.

25

There is talk about artificial intelligence, whether that of computers or of robots, becoming a threat to humans as these machines gain humanlike abilities.

When *everything* about us is being recorded and stored via the Internet of Things, it wouldn't take much for an artificial—or human—intelligence to control us.

There is a scene from *Night Talk* that demonstrates how the Internet of Everything Wrong will work to keep track of us, record forever our every move, and eventually invade our minds. It takes place when radio talk show host Greg Nowell pauses at a closed clothing store late at night and wonders whether a mannequin in the display window knows exactly who he is and everything about him, from his credit rating to his shirt size and the color of his underwear.

> Staring at a mannequin in the window display, he wondered if he was being filmed by a camera in the eye of the dummy. If someone had told him when he was a kid that someday store mannequins would have camera eyes equipped with a facial identification program that told the store salespeople whether he was a returning customer and what his previous purchases were, he'd have thought it was science fiction.

He considers facial recognition one of the most serious electronic dangers to society, and he goes on to discuss a talk he had given about it.

"It bothers me that I have a Big Brother that's always looking over my shoulder . . . One of his nasty little gadgets he's come up with is computer software that identifies a person by viewing their features. Once the person's identity is known, another app gives access to everything available on the Internet about the person in the blink of an eye.

"Facial identification cameras will soon be common wherever I go. Even if it is my first visit to a store, the salespeople will be able to access my history of purchases not only for that store but anywhere I slide a bank card. It irks the hell out of me that a person in a backroom at a store watching a computer screen will know what I eat and drink, read and watch, my preference for clothes and cars. It won't be hard to find out how much I earn and who I make love with.

"If I go into a restaurant, I don't want the waiter to know how I like my steak or what kind of tipper I am or who I was dining with last night."

Although the book is fiction, facial recognition apps and the mannequins with cameras and facial recognition software are *not fiction*—they are already in use. You may come face-to-face with one the next time you enter a clothing store.

Facial recognition, besides being intrusive, can get dangerous.

Someone with a facial recognition app on their phone can spot you on the street, take a surreptitious snapshot of you, run it through the recognition software, and find out everything that is stored about you on the Internet.

The person using the app could be anyone, from someone interested in the victim romantically to a weirdo.

If it's also a hacker, they will get not just your name and your marital status but also your home and work addresses, your bank and other financial information, and *everything* else about you that has been stored anyplace with a connection to the Internet—which is quickly adding up to just about everything about us.

Even without facial recognition software, a hacker with a cell phone can take control of your vehicle's steering, ignition, and brakes; unlock your home and business doors; take command of the commercial jetliner flying you to London; and empty your bank account.

Our government legislates the laws covering computer programming and the purveyors of software that make money off the programs, and it tells us not to worry, that it can protect us.

We are told this even while the computers at the highest levels of government, the military, and global corporations with the financial powers of nations are being hacked into so frequently that it hardly makes the news.

Now here's a real horror story for you: a hacker can alter your medical records while you lie in a hospital bed and prescribe you the wrong dosage of a critical medicine. Or turn off that machine controlling your heart.

Sound like the plot to a TV cop show?

Unfortunately, here again, the truth is stranger than fiction.

THE INTERNET OF EVERYTHING WRONG

"But this Internet of Things is going to be the Internet of Everything Wrong because what you can do a hacker can do. Someone with a fraction of the talent for hacking that I have can walk up to your house with their cell phone and turn off your alarm and open your door. Do you have a system that can turn off your engine remotely if the car's stolen? If you can, so can a hacker. The road rage incidents of the future are going to involve a hacker in the car behind you accessing your car's programing and ramping up the speed of your car while you're driving it, or turning off its brakes, or activating the anti-thief device that causes the car to come to a sudden stop.

"I can go on and on about what low-level hackers can do, but check out this. You don't like people getting access to your computer and your money? Guess what, hacking into your house isn't that complicated. How are you going to like it when a neighbor hacks into that camera system you set up in your house to check on your kids and turns your family into reality show stars? And puts it online with you wandering around in your underwear."

"You heard it from a hacker's mouth," Greg told his audience.

—George Noory, *Night Talk* (2016)

26

A terrifying threat not in the headlines.

The most terrifying threat to our country is one you rarely read about—as if it is too serious to even speak about.

Former president Bill Clinton warned about it.

George W. Bush and Putin were both so concerned that it was enough to bring them together to support a global initiative to prevent it.

Barack Obama called it the single most important national security threat we face.

What causes the concern is the notion of a nuclear weapon falling into the hands of terrorists.

The mental images conveyed by that event happening are gruesome, wherever the nuclear device is set off. As targets are picked, it becomes not just a mind game about how many casualties but also a realization that a single "suitcase nuke," which the U.S. and Russia have developed, could threaten the very foundations of civilization.

An atomic explosion anywhere would be a horrible tragedy, but put it in the heart of New York, London, Paris, Moscow, Tokyo, or any other large city and the death toll would be in the hundreds of thousands.

Precisely target Wall Street, and the national and worldwide financial consequences would affect billions, turn the United States into a third world economy, and perhaps bring down most of the major economies on the planet. A suitcase (or back-pack/knapsack) nuke strategically placed in Washington, DC, would chop the head off our government.

I have focused on small, suitcase-type nukes because they can be easily concealed, transported, smuggled across borders, and strategically placed for maximum damage.

Some people write off the threat by saying that it is too difficult for terrorists to get their hands on a nuclear weapon.

So far, however, terrorists have managed to "get their hand on" all or part of Afghanistan, Syria, Libya, Iraq, Lebanon, and other regions, along with sophisticated weapons of war that permit them to take on troops from the most powerful country in the world and its allies. Obtaining an already-made atomic weapon is hardly beyond their skills, planning, or financial resources.

Russia has had a rusting arsenal of nukes, dating from the Cold War, that at times during the past couple of decades has seemed to be up for sale to the highest bidder.

Pakistan is an even worse scenario, because it is on shaky ground economically and ideologically. There are extremist Islamic elements fighting the government and actively seeking an atomic weapon. During his lifetime, Osama bin Laden actually met with the "father of the Pakistan atomic bomb" to get information on obtaining a bomb. ISIL has also announced that it seeks an atomic weapon to use against the United States.

I have heard people dismiss the threat by saying that the Soviets/Russians have had nukes for decades and have never used them. That assessment ignores a fundamental reason why the bombs that the great powers possess don't get used: the consequences to the *attacker* are guaranteed to be lethal, because it is pretty much a sure thing that if a Russian head of state ordered a nuclear attack on the United States, he or she would also end up dead as part of the retaliation. Even if the Russians were buried so deeply that they actually survived the blasts, the world they stuck their heads out into afterward would be one of radioactive rubble.

The leader of a nation, any nation, would have to be crazy to order an atomic attack on a superpower like the United States, which could and would retaliate. It is even possible to analyze the debris from an atomic explosion and tell where the bomb was manufactured.

The problem is that terrorist leaders are not sane.

That Pakistani government officials and workers can't be trusted makes the war against nuclear terrorists almost impossibly difficult. America's then ambassador to Pakistan, Anne W. Patterson, expressed this frustration in a WikiLeaked memo, in which she said she did not worry about Pakistani terrorists stealing nuclear bomb-fuel as much as she feared government employees smuggling it out, peddling it to terrorists, or constructing a crude terrorist nuke themselves.

—Robert Gleason, *The Nuclear Terrorist* (2014)

PART V

A PERFECT STORM
IS GATHERING

The march of science has taken it into the domain of one of Mother Nature's most powerful elements: *weather*.

Weather is being manipulated.

Secretly.

By unseen hands.

Weather has become a weapon of war.

Of economic control.

With a purpose of world control.

If you control our nation's climate—the life-giving rain for our crops and our thirst—you have a stranglehold on our government and people.

27

Let's talk about the weather.

I know talking about the weather is considered boring. As Oscar Wilde bluntly put it, "Conversation about the weather is the last refuge of the unimaginative."

The advice of suspense novelist Elmore Leonard to fellow writers is to never start a book by talking about the weather. And there's the complaint that people talk about the weather but never do anything about it.

The problem is that there *are* people doing something about the weather—and it's a danger to us individually and as a country.

We'll get to that in a moment, but first we need to get up to speed about what most of us know about what is happening to the weather—including its modification.

Those comments from novelists don't relate to global weather that actually threatens the existence of the human species. Not only is the entire solar system heating up but also, in addition to the forces of the universe, the changes in weather over the past six or seven decades are becoming more and more a threat to our existence—and I'm not just talking about the "global warming" that is in the news so often.

We need to look past what the manipulators of weather want us to see to get at what is really happening. Hopefully, by the time we are done, we might be able to actually do something about it.

What has happened and continues to happen to our weather

and climates is not unlike what has been occurring in recent wars, those bloody terroristic conflicts that appear to be premeditated and manipulated, as if there were a dirty hand in the makings rather than just religious, social, and political animosities going back more than a millennium.

There is no doubt that weather is and has been manipulated. It is easy to prove. We will get to weather modification, how weather is being manipulated, who is doing it, and their dark motives, but first let's deal with the single climate issue that always dominates any discussion of the subject: global warming.

The biggest problem I have always had with global warming is that it has become much more of a political issue than a physical and scientific one. And all sides to the controversy have a tendency not only to politicalize it but also to act as advocates for whichever side they are supporting.

There are those who reject outright the notion that global warming is occurring, those who say it is occurring but that human activities are not a factor in the cause, others who assert that it is occurring and that humans have been aggravating the process for decades or longer. There are even those whose position is that global warming will bring more benefit than harm to the world.

Some things about climate, in general, can be said. Carcinogenic air pollutants are an undeniable problem. No one wants our cities to go the way of Beijing, where people sometimes have to wear masks and noxious silver iodide rains down as part of the city's climate control attempt.

We have often had strange weather in recent times. There is warming of the planet's climate overall, as measured by air and sea temperatures, the melting of snow and ice, and an increase in sea level worldwide.

However you define it and whatever the cause, there is worldwide concern about global warming. It appears evident that if global warming increases, and it appears to be doing so, it could do great harm to us as seas rise and extreme storms wreak destruction, and perhaps may even make significant changes to the global climate.

Although the causes of global warming are still being debated, my own take is that there are some factors that have not gotten enough attention and thus have not been made part of the calculations.

I believe that the world is in a planetary cycle, a long-term period of change taking place over thousands of years.

When you look at the world as a whole, it is easy to see that climate changes do radically alter vast areas. One example is a vast, dry region that was once fertile. Arid deserts of North Africa, the Sahara, and the Middle East were once gardens rather than shifting sand. The Romans fought wars because they considered some of the region to be their breadbasket.

There is talk and debate about global warming causing alteration of ocean currents or wind patterns, bringing about another ice age. Over the eons, world-altering ice ages have come and gone. Science has traced five really big ones, but there have been many smaller ones. The Little Ice Age, which brought cold weather to much of North America and northern Europe for several hundred years, right up to the middle of the nineteenth century, is the most recent to affect us.

The fact is that the planet periodically goes through these cycles.

North Africa and the Middle East was, at one time, a lush region. It had water, trees, and shrubbery and was fertile for crops. Something horrible in terms of climate change radically changed the region.

There is no controversy about what happened, no arguments about whether humans polluted the atmosphere or Mother Nature simply changed things. The fact is that Mother Earth went through a planetary cycle. And, because we are not alone in the universe, we can look around and see the same thing happening on other heavenly bodies flying around the sun. Our solar system is heating up.

Looking at images of the arid badlands of Mars, I get the impression of places in the deserts of North Africa and the Middle East. It seems evident that Mars, at some time in the past, had enough atmosphere and moisture to harbor vegetation. It's gone now, which pretty much makes it a certainty that such radical change can happen to a nearby planet. Mars, by the way, is sometimes the planet closest to Earth.

There is some evidence and scientific opinion that thawing of the Martian ice caps is related to fluctuations to Martian global warming caused by the heat put out by the sun. The issue then arises as to whether Earth's atmosphere and ice caps are subject to the same force and whether the solar heat we are getting has increased and is contributing to or creating global warming.

The sun goes through solar cycles, and there are studies that indicate that solar radiation from the sun has at times increased and at other times dimmed over the past several decades.

Another point of evidence about solar fluctuations changing our global weather is related to that Little Ice Age I mentioned above. For nearly a century, during the heart of that terribly cold era, there was no sunspot activity, leading to the belief that the ice age could have been created by reduced solar heat.

The changes and severe weather due to a general heating up in the solar system reach far beyond Earth and Mars. Way out in the outer limits of the solar system, tiny, frigid Pluto appears to be going through a global warming period. Pluto is mostly made up of rock and ice. Since Pluto's temperature runs close to a chilly −400 degrees Fahrenheit, global "warming" would have a very different meaning on Pluto than how we think of it.

Saturn, a supergiant compared to little dwarf Pluto, suffered a planetwide storm that went on for months in 2011. Jupiter likewise has had storms raging and soaring temperatures, while frozen Triton, Neptune's largest moon, has been heating up, its nitrogen ice turning into gas and making the atmosphere thicker.

It may be that not all planets and moons are heating up, but it also may be that they are and no one has found it because testing hasn't been done.

However you look at the evidence, the fact that so many points in the solar system are suffering a heat effect should at least be accounted for in the global warming analysis for our own planet and in considering the question of how much of global warming is due to planetary and solar fluctuations.

I am not stating that humans don't contribute to global warming. But my instinct is that we are not contributing as much as some sources would want to make us believe.

I think many people who are concerned about climate change are confusing pollution, which nobody wants, with what's really happening to this planet—the sun is getting hotter and heating up the whole solar system. All the other planets are showing an increase in temperature and so are we. This is real.

The climate change is real. We are going through Earth changes but it's not just man-made. Are we contributing to some of it? Maybe. But not as much as people say. Even the pope stepped into the controversy, in 2015, when he declared that there is an alarming warming of the climactic system as a result of the use of fossil fuels and that there is an urgent need to develop sources of renewable energy.

The business of climate change, global warming, is big business, and I'm going to do all I can to let people know we're in an Earth cycle. I believe that this planet goes through cycles. We've had worse Earth changes at many times in history, even during the times of the dinosaurs, and we didn't have factories and plants.

However, there is another area of concern, one that is more pressing than global warming in terms of the near future. The bottom line is that weather is being manipulated and modified. The potential consequences to all of us will be earth-shattering if we don't put a stop to it.

28

Weather is being modified. By "modified," I mean that actions are being taken—some chemical, some more in the realm of the physical sciences—to alter our weather.

Obviously, there has been some form of weather alteration going on for a very long time. People have been tinkering with the weather for more than a century, often getting the results they wanted.

We hear a lot about contrails and "chemtrails," but the fact is that both have been around for more than a century. Since the Second World War, there has been a concentrated effort to change weather to something more desirable, usually to improve agriculture. In many states, especially in regions like Texas and the Southwest, there have been ongoing governmental agencies, and private entities, specifically involved in altering the weather.

As the sophistication of the technology of weather modification grew, so too did the power of those seeking to modify the weather. And something else happened: entities with ambitions far beyond adding a bit of rain to corn or wheat fields or a couple more feet of snow on ski slopes entered the field. Quietly. Clandestinely. And their plans had nothing to do with simple agriculture or commerce.

The motives are infinitely more sinister.

The issue isn't whether someone is monkeying with the weather. We know they are. It is open and obvious. But there is something bigger going on here, something beyond what we see with the naked eye. A deeper, darker twist on the modification of weather by faceless entities with malevolent intent.

If that sounds familiar, it should, because it is no coincidence that, whichever way we turn in analyzing the present state of the world, whether it's war, weather, economics, or political domination, there is a common thread of premeditated criminal manipulation with a single, concentrated purpose in mind: world domination.

I told you at the beginning this was going to be a wild ride, so hang in there as we go into how the weather is being used as a weapon to destroy our country and we look beyond the obvious to the motives and techniques of the manipulators.

29

"Weather modification" occurs when there is an intentional manipulation or alteration of the weather.

Few of us ever think about weather being modified. However, weather modification is being done openly in most states and by the federal government. The United Nations bans weather modification in war, and the United States used it in war before the ban.

It's a safe bet that weather is being altered somewhere on the planet every day. A recent count found that forty countries practice some type of weather modification. And most of us are completely unaware of it unless we have an interest in following that type of news or catch a small article somewhere in the "back pages" of the Internet—or have a thirsty farm.

Agricultural cloud seeding, rainmaking, is the most common variety of weather modification.

Some people think that rainmaking is nothing more than a hustle by con artists, something like an old movie starring Burt Lancaster as a confidence man who swindles drought-stricken farmers out of their life savings.

The general idea behind cloud seeding is to change the amount or even the type of precipitation that falls from clouds. A widely used method is to seed cumulus clouds with silver iodide crystals to increase condensation. Originally, dry ice was used. There must be the right sort of conditions, of course, or we would simply pour rain on all droughts, and that obviously does not happen.

By the way, the Environmental Protection Agency considers silver iodide a hazardous substance and a pollutant. But that is another issue.

The concept of weather modification has been around for a very long time, even if it was just ceremonies by indigenous peoples or bribes to pagan gods. The least desirable method I've heard about was primitive people burying children up to their necks in the hope that rain would fall as the gods cried with sympathy.

However, the nineteenth and early twentieth centuries were times of imaginative individual inventiveness, and theories about putting the weather on a leash were both fantastic and terrifying. There were a number of theories about how to melt the Arctic region to make the land beneath the ice usable. The theories usually involved diverting warm ocean currents to the region. I suppose that, back then, no one worried about cities being flooded by rising sea levels and other worldwide climatic impacts.

Jules Verne, the writer who is considered the father of science fiction, wrote a novel in which the Arctic region was to be melted down by throwing the Earth off its axis—with a resulting disaster, as humans tried to trick Mother Nature.

Based upon reports of rain occurring after massive cannon bombardments during great battles, the U.S. government put a general in charge of inducing rain with the concussion created by aerial explosions of dynamite in hot air balloons. I suppose the theory was to shake the rain out of the clouds, but the results were not conclusive enough to keep the program going.

Cereal manufacturer and inventor Charles William Post also experimented with creating rain through various "concussion" methods, including sending dynamite up on kites. He claimed some success, but apparently not enough to do it as a commercial venture.

One of the most famous incidents of rainmaking occurred in

1915–1916, when the city of San Diego hired a rainmaker named Charles Hatfield to bring a downpour. Hatfield had had some apparent success in the Los Angeles area prior to getting the San Diego job. The fee for success was ten thousand dollars—a lot of money a hundred years ago.

Hatfield's method was to set up a vat on top of a twenty-foot tower and fill it with a secret chemical brew. Whether the rain came from Hatfield's chemical cocktail or a storm occurred coincidentally is a matter of speculation, but the sky opened up and it rained the proverbial "cats and dogs." The heavy rains filled dams and dry riverbeds and kept coming, causing wide-scale flooding and damage as it kept pouring for weeks.

The town refused to pay Hatfield because millions of dollars in damage had occurred, along with a claim of twenty deaths.

How much Hatfield's brew had to do with the massive downpour remains a mystery. The storm did provide him with a golden reputation as a rainmaker, but his future efforts were middling. Some claimed that his greatest talent was as a meteorologist, in that he was only able to perform his magic when a storm was coming anyway.

Weather modification got a boost in the 1940s, when General Electric company scientists created rain by seeding clouds with dry ice. Later it was discovered that silver iodide worked.

The military got involved in storm management—Project Cirrus and Project Stormfury—and spent several decades tinkering with storms, including using cloud seeding in an attempt to weaken hurricanes.

How effective has cloud seeding been? The fact that it has been widely used throughout the world for decades tells us that it is effective, although it's not a cure-all for droughts and in fact may not work well in times of drought because the right type and number of clouds needed are not available.

Not only do many states have weather departments that license and monitor weather modification, which is often done

through cloud seeding, but also both the American Meteorological Society and the World Meteorological Organization, a
United Nations agency, support the fact that, under the right circumstances, cloud seeding can be effective.

My point about cloud seeding is that it lulls us into a false
sense of security about weather modification, because it is familiar to us. But, stepping away from rainmaking for wheat and
cornfields, we find that weather modification is being conducted
in big ways, and even in warfare.

MAKING RAIN WITH CANNONS!

It is not surprising that European American settlers in the Great Plains, dependent on agriculture and plagued by drought, would develop an interest in rainmaking. The earliest attempts involved the concussion method, which was premised on the theory that gunpowder explosions triggered friction and generated nuclei to produce rain. In 1890 Congress appropriated funds to put this theory into practice. The task was given to Gen. Robert St. George Dyrenforth. Experimentation began on the C Ranch in Andrews County, Texas, in 1891 and continued at San Antonio, Texas, in 1892. No rainfall occurred. General Dyrenforth was dubbed "General Dryhenceforth," and the remaining funds appropriated for rainmaking experiments reverted to the Department of the Treasury.

—April L. Whitten, "Rainmaking," *Encyclopedia of the Great Plains*, http://plainshumanities.unl.edu/ encyclopedia/doc/egp.wat.023

30

A great deal of weather modification is being done openly and is getting more and more ambitious—and threatening in a number of ways, even though it is not being kept a secret. The threats include countries accusing each other of "stealing" rain, the creation of biological hazards, and the increasing reliance on tampering with Mother Nature, which in and of itself has the power to destroy worlds.

We'll start with the country most active in modifying the weather. It is also the most populous country on the planet: China, with its billion and a half people. Altering the weather has become so commonplace in China that some regions have come to rely upon it as part of their climate. There is also a perception that the Chinese are working at "washing" the air in places like Beijing, where the air sometimes becomes toxic due to pollution and winds from the Mongolian desert.

Tampering with the weather has become so common in China that Beijing has its own governmental weather modification office.

The Chinese claim to have increased rain over arid regions by firing rockets containing silver iodide into clouds, but the program as a whole is extremely ambitious and goes beyond just rainmaking. In addition to making rain, they tackle prevention of hailstorms, create moisture to combat forest fires, and clean the air of dust and pollution. The Chinese claim that they have used it to create snow and to lower sweltering summer temperatures in order to reduce electricity consumption.

Probably the most publicized control of China's weather was

instituted for the 2008 Summer Olympics. On the morning of the day of the opening ceremonies, the city's meteorological agency, tracking rain clouds, realized there was a high probability that the ceremony would be a washout. To make sure the opening ceremonies of the games were not hit by downpours, the Chinese used thousands of rockets and antiaircraft guns to fire silver iodide into the rain belt and "drain" the clouds of rain before the clouds reached the stadium. There also was a threat of lightning.

It's interesting that the Chinese government treated the weather like an enemy invasion.

China and the United States are not the only countries monkeying with the weather. I mentioned earlier that at least forty countries are partaking in weather modification. In 1986, the Soviet Union modified the weather to keep a horrendous disaster from killing its people—and, in turn, brought hell down on millions of its neighbors.

31

Chernobyl is a name that connotes disaster, tragedy, and even infamy, despite the fact that what occurred there was an accident compounded by human error. It's a name that reminds us of what can go wrong when we build things that we can't always control—and when we fail to keep a rein on our technology, we can create hell on earth.

The Chernobyl disaster was also an incident in which weather modification was used, to the detriment of millions of people—people with no connection to the plant, who received no benefit from it, but who just happened to be in the way when the weather was altered.

The 1986 incident occurred at the Chernobyl Nuclear Power Plant in Ukraine, back in the days when the plant and entire region were still part of the Soviet Union. The facility is close to the border with Belarus, which back then, like Ukraine, was a Soviet republic.

The disaster began during routine systems testing at one of the four reactors at the site. A sudden, unexpected power surge occurred. When an emergency shutdown procedure was activated, an even bigger spike in power occurred and the reactor vessel erupted, followed by steam explosions. Fire broke out, sending clouds of radioactive fallout into the atmosphere. The airborne radioactive materials were carried over large parts of the Soviet Union and Europe, with about 60 percent of it landing in Belarus.

This was a badly handled disaster resulting from numerous mistakes. However, the fact that Belarus, a small territory with about ten million people, got the brunt of the radiation wasn't just due to its proximity to the nuclear facility. As the radioactive fallout was moving in the direction of Moscow and other large cities, the Soviet military used airplanes and artillery to seed clouds with silver iodide, creating rain clouds that "washed" the radioactive particles from the sky—over Belarus, where people reported seeing planes scattering something and a black rain falling.

Four hundred times more radioactive material was released from the Chernobyl disaster than by the atomic bombing of Hiroshima in World War II.

The Soviets originally denied that they had created the radioactive rain that fell on Belarus, but the truth came out over time.

Even though the disaster didn't occur during a time of war, it would have been considered an act of war for the Soviets to deliberately rain hell on Belarus—if Belarus had not been part of the Soviet Union at the time. And it's a good example of the incredible effect that something as simple as cloud seeding could have on millions of people.

We'll return to that premise a little later. For the moment, let's take a look at how the United States used weather modification as an actual weapon of war.

32

War and weather.

Soon after World War II, motivated by the success at altering weather with cloud seeding (not to mention the fact that a Cold War had broken out as soon as the shooting war ended), the United States military establishment became serious about investigating and researching the use of weather modification as a weapon of war. A number of projects were launched, including Project Cirrus and Project Stormfury, mentioned previously.

In 1996, U.S. Air Force personnel did a study at the request of the air force chief of staff to examine what would be required for the air force to remain the dominant air and space fighting force in the future. Looking forward to what would be needed by the year 2025, the study focused on control of the weather, and the report was aptly called *Weather as a Force Multiplier: Owning the Weather in 2025.*

The report to the high command was that, by 2025, the United States can "own the weather" by focusing on the development of weather modification technologies. The country that "owns the weather," the report says, "offers the war fighter tools to shape the battlespace in ways never before possible." The report went on to infer that control of the weather is akin to control of atomic weapons:

A high-risk, high-reward endeavor, weather-modification offers a dilemma not unlike the splitting of the atom. While some segments of society will always be reluctant to examine controversial issues such as weather modification, the tremendous military capabilities that could result from this field are ignored at our own peril. From enhancing friendly operations or disrupting those of the enemy via small-scale tailoring of natural weather patterns to complete dominance of global communications and counterspace control, weather-modification offers the war fighter a wide-range of possible options to defeat or coerce an adversary.

The report gives a chilling scenario that makes it hard to ignore its recommendation to take charge of the weather: if the United States doesn't get the lead, some other country will.

I noted earlier that the United States had been working on developing weather for military use since the 1940s, fifty years before the *Owning the Weather* report was made. What the report doesn't mention is that the United States had already conducted large-scale military weather modifications with the technology available at the time. During the Vietnam War, starting in 1967, extensive cloud seeding was used as part of an offensive called Operation Popeye. The objective was to increase precipitation and extend Vietnam's tropical monsoon season, thus disrupting the Ho Chi Minh trail that the North Vietnamese used as a supply line to get war materials to the South.

The entire region was engulfed by the project—the flights for the seeding came out of Thailand, and the seeding was done over Cambodia, Laos, and Vietnam. Silver iodide and lead iodide were used in the seeding. The program ran for about five years, from 1967 to 1972, and was considered a success because the seeding extended the monsoon annually for a month or more and caused flooding.

The U.S. Air Force also used weather control in 1968, during the Battle of Khe Sanh, in an attempt to reduce the fog and cloud cover that hindered air operations bringing supplies to marines during the fighting. C-123 military transport planes flew fifteen missions out of Da Nang to drop salt in an attempt to clear Khe Sanh's fog, but the attempt failed.

The use of weather as a weapon by the United States—even as a rather primitive one, considering it was basically only cloud seeding—exposed fears of what could happen if a country got a hold on controlling the weather.

The result was a 1977 international treaty, the Environmental Modification Convention, formally called the Convention on the Prohibition of Military or Any Other Hostile Use of Environmental Modification Techniques. It prohibits the use of "environmental modification" techniques that have widespread, long-lasting, or severe effects.

Despite the fact that the United States became a party to the treaty, in 1996 the air force was investigating ways to control the planet's weather and use it as a weapon of war—again, citing the rather reasonable assumption that if we didn't do it, someone else would.

Given that the "someone else" was probably going to be an enemy of the United States and most of the rest of the world, with evil motives, I can't say that I disagree with the premise.

But the downside is that it puts us in an arms race similar to the Cold War atomic arms race, which for decades could have caused worldwide nuclear holocaust if someone pushed the wrong button.

Which is pretty much what is going on today, except that today's enemy is not as visible as the Soviets were.

WEATHER AS A WEAPON OF WAR

The lessons of history indicate a real weather-modification capability will eventually exist despite the risk. The drive exists. People have always wanted to control the weather and their desire will compel them to collectively and continuously pursue their goal. . . . History also teaches that we cannot afford to be without a weather-modification capability once the technology is developed and used by others. Even if we have no intention of using it, others will. To call upon the atomic weapon analogy again, we need to be able to deter or counter their capability with our own. Therefore, the weather and intelligence communities must keep abreast of the actions of others. . . .

[W]eather-modification is a force multiplier with tremendous power that could be exploited across the full spectrum of war-fighting environments. From enhancing friendly operations or disrupting those of the enemy via small-scale tailoring of natural weather patterns to complete dominance of global communications and counter-space control, weather-modification offers the war fighter a wide-range of possible options to defeat or coerce an adversary. . . . [I]t is clear that we cannot afford to allow an adversary to obtain an exclusive weather-modification capability.

—Tamzy J. House et al., *Weather as a Force Multiplier: Owning the Weather in 2025* (August 1996)

33

Let's take a look at the project that many "conspiracy theorists" believe is the most important and dangerous weather modification program known—and see how it connects to the 1996 report on owning the weather. It concerns HAARP.

HAARP stands for High Frequency Active Auroral Research Program.

Wow. That is a mouthful. And it's the last time I will call the program by its full name.

HAARP is a U.S. military program dating back to the early 1990s. It's located in the middle of nowhere in Alaska—literally. The closest town, Gakona, has about two hundred residents, and it's also in the middle of nowhere. Being someplace where there's not much evidence of "civilization" is pretty much how the residents of our incredibly wild and scenic wonderland state like it, and I don't blame them.

The government claims that HAARP's goal is to analyze the ionosphere and to ascertain the potential for ionospheric enhanced technology for radio communications and surveillance. The ionosphere is the region of Earth's atmosphere extending from the stratosphere to the exosphere. It's a zone about 37 to 620 miles above our planet's surface and consists of several ionized layers.

Wow. Another mouthful. And I'm not going to bother trying to explain what it means, because life is too short for some things. Suffice it to say, HAARP ranks highly, in the eyes of many conspiracy theorists, as a clandestine weather and communications control program.

After investigating the claims and counterclaims, I have to admit that I also do not buy the military's whitewash of its activities. This is especially true because, after twenty years of deny, deny, deny, a HAARP representative admitted on the record at a congressional hearing that the program has been dealing with the weather.

Situations in which the government is found to have lied are a good reason why people suspect its motives. It reminds me a bit of the Roswell incident, in which the government contended for decades that the alleged UFO wreckage was nothing more than a weather balloon, and then finally admitted that it wasn't a weather balloon but still denied it was a UFO.

Some people dismiss claims that our government is willing to lie to its people to protect its interests, sometimes for good reasons, other times for reasons that turn out, historically, to be flawed. But just because a notion gets labeled as a "conspiracy theory," because the government issues a denial, doesn't always mean that it isn't true.

The uproar about HAARP came in 2014, more than twenty years after the program was established and the government kept denying that it was involved in anything except harmless atmospheric research of the ionosphere.

While we have talked a great deal about altering weather with cloud seeding, a more advanced method being developed is to do it electromagnetically. That is important, because the use of electromagnetism is the way HAARP would do it if it was altering weather. A major claim about using electromagnetics to control weather comes out of incredibly oil-rich Abu Dhabi in the United Arab Emirates. In 2010, heavy rainstorms were created by scientists using ionizing towers. It is claimed that sometimes rain appeared right after the ionizers were turned on.

The admission that HAARP had been involved in ionic

injections into the atmosphere came during a congressional hearing during which a deputy assistant secretary of the air force for science, technology, and engineering was explaining why the air force planned to close the HAARP facility. The air force official told an Alaskan senator, "We're moving on to other ways of managing the ionosphere, which the HAARP was really designed to do. To inject energy into the ionosphere to be able to actually control it. But that work has been completed."

To understand why that statement reveals so much about what people (i.e., conspiracy theorists) who believed the program was designed to control weather and global communications got right, we need to look at what HAARP and others have said about controlling the weather.

To begin with, HAARP's response to "conspiracy theories" about its intentions had always been that it was nothing more than an ionosphere radio science research facility. That was what it told the American public, and that is what it told the European Union when that organization questioned the environmental risks it believed the project was generating in the ionosphere.

However, the air force's *Owning the Weather* report specifically found that the ionosphere's "space weather" was playing an important role in its recommendations for gaining control over the weather and communications.

A year after the air force report was tendered, at a Department of Defense news briefing, then Secretary of Defense William Cohen laid out the situation in plain language, stating that there was an effort by "some countries" to use the weather as a weapon, and that those countries were "engaging even in an eco-type of terrorism whereby they can alter the climate, set off earthquakes, volcanoes remotely through the use of electromagnetic waves. . . . So there are plenty of ingenious minds out there that are at work finding ways in which they can wreak terror upon other nations. It's real, and that's the reason why we have to intensify our efforts, and that's why this is so important."

Weather is both thermal and electromagnetic, as the people in Abu Dhabi learned. HAARP admitted it was in the business of using electromagnetism to control and energize the atmosphere, while the secretary of defense is saying that the threat to America is from weather manipulation through electromagnetics.

Now we know why that air force official's statement to Congress in 2014 is so damning to HAARP's decades-long denial that it was involved in weather manipulation. The air force official quoted above said, in essence, that HAARP was "really designed" as a way of "managing the ionosphere," to "inject energy into the ionosphere to be able to actually control it," and that HAARP's "work has been completed." Meaning, of course, that it had accomplished its mission.

Atomic bombs, hydrogen bombs, the biggest and the baddest weapons that we have come up with, do not even compare in the slightest to the widespread destructive power of hurricanes, floods, earthquakes, and tornadoes.

To control the weather is to control the planet.

That fact brings us to the bottom line on weather control. It's a conclusion I don't like.

34

Weather as a force of conquest.

The Bible tells of many cataclysmic events, ranging from wiping the whole slate clean with a flood to fire and brimstone from the sky.

The wrath of Mother Nature has the ability to bring devastation of biblical proportions to us. Not even atomic warfare would be likely to destroy everything on the planet. But, like the Death Star, the Empire's planet-killing space base in *Star Wars*, Mother Nature has the ability to destroy every living thing, every man-made thing, even nature's own beautiful and mighty things, and has the ability to turn the planet into a ball of ice, an endless ocean, or shatter and scatter it entirely.

Weather, a force of nature, can be one of nature's most destructive forces. To harness it, to control and be able to modify it, is a power of biblical proportions, a weapon with the immense power of the Ark of the Covenant.

Global warming and climate change of any kind is a slow process. Its effect is measured in decades, centuries, even millennia. Weather modification can be in your face, right now.

Some use of weather modification in warfare is easily imagined—causing massive logistics problems through heavy rain and floods, for example. A much more subtle but incredibly brutal and effective way would be to go after the opposing country itself and not just its armed forces. What are those three common disasters nature inflicts so often? Flood, famine, and fire.

Drought and floods not only could achieve uncomfortable

and dangerous conditions for the general population (remember Hatfield's rainstorms, which paralyzed the region, breaking dams and levees) but also could destroy food supplies and the ability to produce food. Nature's own electrical storms over forests create fires that destroy millions of acres. Unleashing man-made lightning could increase those fires manyfold.

Weather can be so destructive that it is absolutely the last thing we want to be under the control of mankind. If it does come under the control of an entity on the planet, it would be catastrophic for it to be in the "wrong" hands. This includes almost everyone, but terrorists, rogue states, and nations that spend most of their time teetering on the brink of social and political upheaval obviously jump instantly onto the short list.

We know dozens of countries, including our own, are working at controlling weather. It is obvious that what Abu Dhabi is doing to stimulate rain in the desert and China to relieve droughts are only the tip of what is going on.

We have to assume that countries with the technical ability and financial means are working on ways to take control of the weather. The United States, China, and Russia would have the largest programs. And we have to assume that whatever gets into the hands of one entity will end up in the hands of terrorists and rogue states, just as terrorists and rogue states have attempted to get atomic weapons.

As I pointed out earlier, HAARP's work on the ionosphere and the air force's 1996 report stressing the need for our country to "own the weather" are clear indications that we have been involved in investigating control of the weather as a military force for decades.

There is so much at stake in this race, so much chance that the forces of evil could get control of an invincible weapon, that we need to put every possible effort into getting it first.

My feeling is that it is not just great powers like the United States and China that are attempting to gain control of the weather. I sense that the same shadowy, clandestine manipulator involved in the control of war, politics, and society also is seeking control of this weapon of biblical proportions.

It comes as no surprise to me that the United Nations, through its World Meteorological Organization, is involved in weather modification. It fits nicely with its aim for a One World Government and a weakened America.

PART VI

WATER AND WAR

The competition for "blue gold" is already creating wars. Just as wildcatters made great fortunes finding "black gold" and nations fought wars over oil, water is becoming "the stuff that dreams are made of."

As our national and global supply of water diminishes, nations are already fighting to control the supply, while businesspeople call it blue gold and lust to control it for profit. Water has entered the marketplace and is treated as a "commodity" like oil, corn, and wheat—a product to own and control, to price according to supply and demand, at the highest price the market will bear.

Good Lord! This "product" is a natural substance as important to us as the air we breathe.

GLOBAL CONFLICT OVER WATER

The world is at war over water. Goldman Sachs describes it as "the petroleum of the next century." Disputes over water tend to start small and local. . . . But minor civil unrest can quickly mushroom, as the bonds of civilization snap.

It is often forgotten that the revolution against Syrian president Bashar al-Assad began this way, when youths of the southern Syrian town of Daraa, angry at the local governor's corrupt allocation of scarce reservoir water, were caught spraying anti-establishment graffiti. Their arrest and torture was the final straw for the tribes from which the youths came. It was a very similar story in Yemen, whose revolution began in 2011 in Taiz, the most water-stressed city in that country. . . .

—James Fergusson, "The World Will Soon Be at War Over Water," *Newsweek* (April 24, 2015)

35

A 1974 movie selected by the National Film Registry for preservation in the Library of Congress as being "culturally, historically, or aesthetically significant" was inspired by a famous water war. The film, *Chinatown*, starring Jack Nicholson, also has been selected by the American Film Institute as one of the best mystery movies ever made.

The film didn't actually deal with the water war but it was inspired by the conflict. Sometimes true events are stranger than fiction, and this is one of those cases.

One character in the film is William Mulholland, the head of the Los Angeles water department, who ignited an explosive conflict with farmers and ranchers in Inyo County's Owens Valley, about 250 miles from Los Angeles, when he turned the valley into a desert by taking its water. The dispute was called the California Water Wars. It began before World War I and turned explosive during the 1920s as the Owens Valley farmers and ranchers saw their livelihoods flowing away to satisfy the thirst of Angelenos.

Mulholland rode high as the genius who brought water at any cost—*from other regions*—to fuel the incredible growth of arid Los Angeles, until he made a deadly engineering mistake on a dam.

The Saint Francis Dam was built to store water taken from Owens Valley. The farmers and ranchers battling Mulholland had used dynamite several times to disrupt what they considered to be theft of their precious water. When the Saint Francis

Dam was newly finished, the police received reports that the water warriors were going to blow it up.

Blowing up the new dam never proved necessary. Instead, soon after completion, the dam burst all on its own, flooding a wide area and killing between three hundred and fifty and four hundred people. It broke hours after Mulholland had checked it and declared it was in no danger.

The 1928 catastrophe is considered one of the worse engineering disasters in U.S. history, and in California it ranks second only to the 1906 San Francisco earthquake in terms of loss of life.

Suffice it to say, it ruined Mulholland's career. But he got a world famous street and another dam named after him.

36

Historically, wars happen for many reasons—religion, treasure, and territory are pretty common. In ancient times, a mighty king or pharaoh might attack a weaker nation just to enslave thousands to build monuments to his ego.

We know that, in modern times, lust for oil, or black gold, has replaced the lust for actual gold as a reason for war.

Now our national security people tell us that a new "treasure," greedily sought, which will cause global instability and threaten the United States, is blue gold—water.

Water and war. What a terrible combination. It sounds worse than wars over food, because when it's not available, water is a more urgent, immediate need than even food. We hear from survivalists that you can last weeks without food but only days without water. Under the worst circumstances, you may last only hours, rather than days, without water.

The need for water and food are infinitely more pressing and critical than the need for oil. You can last forever without petroleum—unless someone kills you for it.

There are many ways in which war and water are linked, but we don't recognize the connection because there are so many other things going on. The conflicts in the world's hot-bed of chaos, the Middle East, are a good example.

The Israeli–Palestinian conflict has been going on for decades. They have been fighting over religion and land, right? Yes, that's true. But it's not the whole truth. It is also about water.

The Jordan River is as familiar a name to most Americans

as the Mississippi and the Colorado because of the role it played in Judaism and Christianity. Jesus, John the Baptist, and the Sea of Galilee are biblical names that immediately make connections to the river.

The river also runs through a hotbed of conflict. That "West Bank" we hear so much about is the west side of the Jordan River. And the Golan Heights are another key area with regard to the river and its tributaries.

It would obviously be a major blow to Israel if water from the Jordan were cut off. Although the Six-Day War of 1967 was fought for many reasons, former Israeli prime minister Ariel Sharon put water as the major reason, because Syria and other Arab entities attempted to divert the flow. The water issues may date back to the 1960s and beyond, but it still creates violent tensions in the region.

The Jordan River doesn't hold a monopoly on creating conflict and tension in the Middle East and adjoining areas. Tensions among Turkey, Syria, and Iraq are caused by disputes over the Euphrates and the Tigris, those "cradle of civilization" waterways; Egypt, Sudan, and Ethiopia have disagreements about the Nile; former Soviet republics in Central Asia argue over the Caspian and Aral Seas; and India and Pakistan have disputes about the waters of Kashmir.

All of these tensions and more destabilize the world and add to our own security woes, because most of the nations involved have little superstructure to handle the crises that arise due to drought or water being diverted. Almost all of the nations involved in water disputes are third world nations, handicapped by poverty and inefficient and ineffectual governments.

Take, for example, one of the warring phenomena of our time: ISIS and its murderous rituals. Here, again, we hear a great deal about religious conflict among Islamic factions. What we don't hear about is the water issue that contributed to the collapse of the Syrian nation and the rise of a grotesque terrorist entity. What occurred in Syria was a long drought, which brought misery and hunger in farming areas and drove people into cities, creating more poverty. The regime of President Bashar al-Assad failed to stabilize the country, and the result was an ever-widening civil war between the government and various factions—one of which was ISIS.

One statistic explains much of the problem: the Middle East contains 5 percent of the world's population but only 1 percent of its water.

WATER AT FIRE SALE PRICES?

The existence of a private company that owns and sells as a commodity the water we need for our very existence reminds me of the way in which public services were conducted in ancient Rome. It gives a different meaning to the term "fire sale."

Services like the police, fire department, and rubbish collection were partitioned out to wealthy Romans, who provided these services to the city and made a profit doing it.

Rome's first significant fire department was created by a wealthy individual named Crassus, who was born rich and became much richer, according to Roman historian Plutarch, through "fire and rapine."

Because the city lacked a fire department, Crassus created one with five hundred men, mostly slaves. When a cry of fire arose, Crassus's fire brigade rushed to the burning building and lined up at the nearest water source to hand buckets from one to the other—as soon as the price for services was met.

If the property owner met Crassus's price, the fire was attacked. But if the owner wouldn't pay up, the building was allowed to burn, while the frantic owners of nearby buildings negotiated with Crassus.

Sometimes Crassus simply bought the burning buildings—at "fire sale" prices.

37

We've talked about water as a source of war that threatens our security. Unfortunately, it has also become a weapon of war.

Water has long played a role in war, in addition to being the bottom line reason for conflict. In ancient and medieval times, cities were built next to rivers as often as possible, not only for the water but also to make it more difficult to attack. Castles had moats. Stopping or poisoning the water supply was always a favorite weapon of siege. And, as we learned from the movie *Lawrence of Arabia*, a dispute over a well in the desert would be settled by gunfire.

We don't need to look further than the California Water Wars to see that we aren't much different from those bedouins when it comes to protecting our water supply. As Mark Twain said after a trip through the parched Western states, in the West, "whiskey is for drinking; water is for fighting over."

Things have not changed much over the millennia. Using water as a weapon to beat one's enemy is still a tactic of war.

During the Arab Spring civil war that broke out in Libya, Gaddafi's forces went medieval: they cut off water to the capital, Tripoli, and other cities. This left a large part of the country without water, and the international community came to the rescue with tanker ships carrying water. In Syria and Iraq, ISIS repeatedly used water as a weapon, cutting off water in fights for Aleppo, Syria, and Fallujah in Iraq's Anbar province. The Syrian government also has gotten into the act, bombing water sources.

It's no wonder that U.S. intelligence sources, analyzing

issues that raise the prospect of war and disputes in third world countries around the world, and that jeopardize our own country's security, see conflicts over water as so pressing.

One of the key issues is that there is little prospect of countries in the Middle East getting together and participating in transnational cooperation for the distribution and use of the most important resource they possess. This reality, that the countries that most need to cooperate are incapable of it, is aggravated by another fact of singular importance to all of us: the world is running out of fresh water. And we are not immune to this hydrological disaster.

We must treat the physical world that we depend upon for our survival with the same care that we give to our own bodies.

BUG-KILLING BOOK

Once in a while I hear about something that leaves me amazed at the cleverness and usefulness of it. Hearing about this one, in the context of hundreds of millions of people having no access to clean, healthy water, is fantastic.

Clever scientists have developed a "book" with special pages that have silver or copper ions embedded in the paper and instructions on how to take out a page and use it to remove harmful bacteria from water.

You simply tear out the page and fold it into a shape not unlike the cones used in many coffeemakers. You then pour the water from a stream, lake, or wherever into the cone. As the water seeps through the paper, the bacteria absorb the silver or copper ions embedded in the paper and are killed. When the water comes out, it is as clean as most of the public drinking water in the United States. One of these specially manufactured "books" could provide an individual's drinking water for four years.

At the time of this writing, the process is still being tested, but it appears to be extremely promising.

38

A perfect storm is on the horizon. It's a disaster that will happen if climate change continues to reduce the supply of fresh water and other vital resources and we reach a tipping point. Our intelligence agencies call it a "resource shock."

As we've seen, water has been called "blue gold" for good reasons. It is a magic elixir. Like people and planets and everything else we see in the visible universe, it is made of star stuff, debris left over from the big bang—or however else it all came into being. It is the basis of life on Earth. It is what we are searching for on other planets to find out if we indeed are all alone in the universe.

Like the black gold that fuels our wars and our greed, or like wheat, water is being turned into a "commodity."

How much water do we have? Actually, I think a better question is how much *fresh water* do we have, because 97.5 percent of the water on Earth is found in the oceans. Fresh water accounts for just 2.5 percent, and more than two-thirds of that is in the form of glaciers and permafrost. Almost a third of the 2.5 percent is groundwater, which requires more effort to get than what is on the surface. That leaves about four-tenths of one percent (0.4 percent) of the water on the planet in our lakes, rivers, and other surface sources.

Here's another statistic: agriculture uses 93 percent of the fresh water; industry and domestic uses account for the remaining 7 percent.

Thus, only a tiny part of the water on the planet is fresh water, and only a small part of that is easily obtained, because most of it is frozen—and more than 90 percent of what we do use goes to grow our food.

What all these statistics convey to me is that my mental image of a planet with 70 percent of its surface covered with blue oceans has little to do with the water that is piped into my home.

Part of the problem is not how much precipitation falls but where it falls. Some areas, like frigid Antarctica, the Arctic, and Greenland, get lots of water. So do the tropics. But there are great swatches of the planet, in between, where things are drying up.

In recent times, California and other states have suffered from drought and diminishing water supplies, but even as droughts come and go, the world as a whole has fresh water problems because of the demands of populations that have increased by the billions over the decades, because of water-intensive industries erupting in places where there was empty land before, and because a great deal of drinkable water is being contaminated by people and industrial waste.

One study, using data collected by NASA satellites over a decade (from 2003 to 2013), analyzed the world's largest aquifers. An aquifer is where we find underground water when we dig a well. As we have seen, it is also where about a third of the fresh water on the planet is found. The analysis revealed a startling fact: twenty-one of the thirty-seven largest aquifers on the planet have gone beyond their "sustainability tipping points." That means more water is being drawn from these underground reservoirs than is being replenished by rain or snowmelt. If we keep using the underground water and it doesn't get replenished, we will run out of it.

These vast groundwater reservoirs have taken thousands (or millions?) of years to fill. With modern machinery, we are quickly emptying them. We have gone from thousands of years of human existence in which wells were shallow to being able to drill deep and suck out water by the millions of gallons. In the past century or so, we have gone from hardly using deep groundwater to the point where about 35 percent of the fresh water used on the planet comes from aquifers.

Water is being treated as a commodity. Smart billionaires and mega financial institutions are buying up water sources to turn blue gold into dollars. In some third world areas, the drinkable water supply becomes something like using an ATM to withdraw cash.

That perfect storm I mentioned is on the horizon, because no matter what we feel are the causes of global warming, we are in an Earth cycle in which the planet and the whole solar system are heating up. One of the scary things about drought is that not only are we not getting a normal amount of precipitation but also, because of the heat generated, our need for water can increase while Mother Nature supplies less.

Remember, agriculture uses up 90 percent of our fresh water. When our intelligence agencies talk about the resource shock that's coming, they are referring to the fact that one problem leads to another: more global heat, less water, less food, more unrest, more wars.

Close to a billion people on the planet don't have access to clean water. What's going to happen when even more don't have access to any water and hundreds of millions become "climate refugees"? This is what Director of National Intelligence James Clapper said about the situation, in 2015:

Many countries important to the United States are vulnerable to natural resource shocks that degrade economic development, frustrate attempts to democratize, raise the risk of regime-threatening instability, and aggravate regional tensions. Extreme weather events (floods, droughts, heat waves) will increasingly disrupt food and energy markets, exacerbating state weakness, forcing human migrations, and triggering riots, civil disobedience, and vandalism.

SHOULD WE BE RATIONING OUR NATIONAL RESOURCES?

"Rationing" sounds like something done during times when resources become more scarce than ordinarily, as frequently happens during times of war or drought. But analyses by the national intelligence director and private think tanks raise a good question: should individual countries set a quota for their use of national resources, such as water and forests, so they don't use more each year than is replenished by Mother Nature?

With that "perfect storm" of ecological disaster on the horizon, we should start getting used to using only what we have, rather than continuing to create "needs" that exceed what can be replenished.

This is another ticking bomb that our elected leaders don't want to deal with, because there are no easy answers.

39

Is abiotic oil an unlimited supply of oil?

I mentioned earlier that, on my show, I like to look at news and issues from different angles rather than just accepting the status quo, if there is a basis for exploring further. Rather than just reporting the situation, I strive to broaden our perspective by analyzing events, situations, and news stories, and looking beyond conventional wisdom. I do that in many different realms, including science.

Using that approach, the results can often be surprising, because we learn much more as we reach deeper with questions.

While we are speaking of how water is catching up with oil as a source of conflict and greed, let's take a look at what could be a vast, untouched supply of petroleum sitting right under our feet. The existence of plenty of oil, rather than a limited supply that we are quickly diminishing, may sound like a fantasy, but there is a substantial scientific theory behind the concept.

The issue is whether there is abiotic oil—petroleum that is not a product of living organisms.

The oil we pull from the ground is called fossil fuel because it was created by the decay of massive amounts of biomass, the remains of organisms dead for millions of years. In a simplistic view, probably inspired by a picture in a grammar school geology textbook when I was a kid, I imagine vast swamps, with dinosaurs and other giant animals stomping around, the swamps and animals getting buried by titanic geologic forces.

We know where oil comes from—for sure, it's beneath us.

But the question arises about whether, very deep in the bowels of Earth, there are vast reservoirs of oil that wasn't produced by once-living organisms. Some outstanding scientists believe in the existence of such abiotic oil, and I am not willing to reject the concept while there are still questions.

We hear about the price of oil more often than we hear about the price of milk or bread, and what we hear doesn't always make a lot of sense to consumers: if the price of oil goes up, it's bad for the economy; if the price goes down, it's bad for the economy.

Sometimes it seems as if it's more a question of what the powers in control want the effect to be.

Whatever it is, oil keeps the gears of our planet moving.

And we know that it is a diminishing resource that someday will no longer be available. But is that the end of the story? It is if you accept without question that the sole source of oil is from biomass that has been compressed and buried over millions of years.

The alternative concept is that Earth's vast crude oil reservoirs are not the product of the decay of organic matter but were created deep in the planet, by tremendous pressure, under ultrahot conditions. Under the abiotic (nonbiological) theory, oil has been pushed up from the core of the planet and there is a lot more of it than we suspect—perhaps an unlimited supply.

The first problem one gets into when discussing how oil is created is that, like the controversy over global warming, there are political and economic ramifications that go beyond scientific debate. There are vested interests: it is to the benefit of the major oil producing companies that oil is thought of as a diminishing, nonrenewable resource. Making sure oil is accepted as scarce and expensive enables control of price and production.

The notion that oil is fossil fuel created from ancient biomass is the most generally accepted theory, but the proponents of abiotic oil are also impressive. Russian and Ukrainian scientists have long contended that oil is not fossil fuel but is created in Earth's innards and is impregnated by living matter as it seeps up. Those scientists had a prominent American scientist who agreed with them: Dr. Thomas Gold, a distinguished astrophysicist.

There also was an oil reservoir event that brought a great deal of attention to the theory that oil is pushed up from Earth's hot interior rather than pressed down as a biomass. The oil field in question was thought to have been mostly pumped, when it suddenly received an influx of more oil—from below.

Also, analysis of chemical data obtained from other planets reveals that methane, a hydrocarbon, is present on other planets and on asteroids that have never supported living matter.

There is no easy resolution to the controversy. It may be that both theories are in fact correct and that there is more than one way for oil to be created. And, as consumers, we care more about the price and availability than the science, anyway. But those of us who believe the abiotic theory have good reason to say it needs to be further pursued: it can affect the price and availability of the oil we so rely upon.

PART VII

WE ARE NOT ALONE

We know they're out there!

We can prove it!

I'm talking about extraterrestrials. It's a subject that many people will avoid out of fear of ridicule—or just a lack of knowledge about the prospect of other "life" existing in our universe. Existing even on our planet.

To protect ourselves we have to stop denying it.

Survival may depend upon who—and what—we will be dealing with.

The late Carl Sagan put it well on his show *Cosmos*: "By exploring other worlds we safeguard this one. By itself, I think this fact more than justifies the money our species has spent in sending ships to other worlds. It is our fate to live during one of the most perilous and, at the same time, one of the most hopeful chapters in human history."

40

When I was fourteen, my mother got me a book I had asked for. Called *We Are Not Alone*, it was written by Walter Sullivan, a *New York Times* science editor. Using strong data and drawing conclusions from science, Sullivan set out the case that we earthlings are not alone in the universe, that we should face the inevitable and understand that there are other forms of life "out there," and that there even may be something—or someone—in the beyond that is far more technologically advanced than us.

The book was controversial and provocative at the time—more than half a century ago—because of its premise that there is life in the universe besides us earthlings.

What a mind-blowing concept for an adolescent who was already curious about the strange and unexplainable. I read the book with breathless excitement. This man, a distinguished commentator on science, said there are extraterrestrials, *aliens*, somewhere out there in the stars.

In essence, he was saying that the extraterrestrials and spacecraft found in cheap pulp magazines and low-low-budget movies with bad acting, ridiculous special effects, and comical space suits were real. They are out there, ready to be discovered—or for them to discover us!

Being fascinated by the subject of extraterrestrials and alien worlds was one thing, but I also had to make sure I was not blinded by it.

Over the years, I have looked not just at what was claimed and what was debunked but also at the evidence that clearly indicates that we are not alone in the universe, and that we even have had extraterrestrial contact right here on our own planet.

In the book, Sullivan laid out earlier conceptions of the universe and how they were revised over time as science began making holes in concepts people had held for thousands of years. He showed how organic matter, the essentials for life as we know it, is spread through the universe, and he theorizes about some of the consequences of encountering extraterrestrial life-forms.

As Carl Sagan put it on *Cosmos*, humans—you and I and the people next door, each and every one of us—are part and parcel of the universe; we are literally made from stardust.

The surface of the Earth is the shore of the cosmic ocean. On this shore, we've learned most of what we know. Recently, we've waded a little way out, maybe ankle-deep, and the water seems inviting. Some part of our being knows this is where we came from. We long to return, and we can, because the cosmos is also within us. We're made of star stuff. We are a way for the cosmos to know itself. . . . We are star stuff which has taken its destiny into its own hands.

That we are "star stuff," that the elements used in the chemistry of life were originally synthesized in stars, is a marvelous, magical way to describe our cosmic connection.

NASA has spent decades since Sullivan's book investigating whether or not we are alone in the universe. The facts and data assembled by NASA pretty much make it a certainty that there is life beyond this planet.

Why is it so important, so vital for us as human beings to find out if there is someone else out there?

We know intelligent life exists in the universe. Jokes aside about how "intelligent" humans are, we have a vast and varied array of life right here on the blue planet. There are a zillion varieties: things that swim, wiggle, crawl, walk, run, and fly; ones living under incredible pressure on the bottom of the deepest oceans, in fiery volcanoes, under mile-deep ice, in our outer atmosphere, and in vents spewing poison that would kill any other living thing on the planet.

We know life can exist under extremes here on Earth, but how do we know there is life beyond us—ideally something other than microbes; a life-form that can communicate with us, that we can learn from, and that can learn from us?

Partly it has to do with simple numbers. Our planet is an infinitesimal speck, not even a tiny grain of sand, in a universe so vast that it is immeasurable in every direction. The odds of intelligent life among not just billions but trillions of planets are too high to dismiss.

They are out there, in that illimitable vastness of space, scattered among the uncountable stars.

Who and what they are is a serious issue.

Before we go deeper into the search for and evidence of extraterrestrial life, I want to address a good question that gets occasionally posed: Why should we be looking for life beyond Earth?

The universe that lies about us, visible only in the privacy, the intimacy of night, is incomprehensibly vast. Yet the conclusion that life exists across the vastness seems inescapable. We cannot yet be sure whether or not it lies within reach, but in any case we are part of it all; we are not alone!

—Walter Sullivan, *We Are Not Alone* (1964)

41

Both Walter Sullivan and Carl Sagan point out that it is in our nature both to ask questions and to find answers to the unknown and to the mysteries of life.

Sullivan appeals to the adventurers we humans are, telling us that we need to fire up that sense of daring and exploration that sent brave people off to find "new worlds" so many times:

The world desperately needs a global adventure to rekindle the flame that burned so intently during the Renaissance, when new worlds were being discovered on our own planet and in the realms of science. Within a generation or less we will vicariously tread the moon and Mars, but the possibility of ultimately "seeing" worlds in other solar systems, however, remote, is an awesome prospect. . . .

The realization that life is probably universal, however thinly scattered through the universe, has meaning for all who contemplate the cosmos and the mortality of man. . . . Life, in a sense, may be eternal. Perhaps true wisdom is a torch—one that we have not yet received, but that can be handed on to us by a civilization late in its life and passed on by our own world as its time of extinction draws near.

Thus, as our children and grandchildren offer some continuity to our personal lives, so our communion with cosmic manifestations of life would join us with a far more magnificent form of continuity.

In his book *Cosmos* (1980), Carl Sagan, the brilliant scientist and dreamer, appealed to our sense of mystery about who and what we are:

> As long as there have been humans, we have searched for our place in the Cosmos. . . . Where are we? Who are we? We find that we live on an insignificant planet of a hum-drum star . . . a galaxy . . . tucked away in some forgotten corner of a universe in which there are far more galaxies than people. . . .
>
> We embarked on our journey to the stars with a question first framed in the childhood of our species and in each generation asked anew with undiminished wonder: What are the stars? Exploration is in our nature. We began as wanderers, and we are wanderers still. We have lingered long enough on the shores of the cosmic ocean. We are ready at last to set sail for the stars.

The flame of adventure . . . Wanderers . . . On the shores of the cosmic ocean . . . Ready to set sail for the stars . . .

When I read what these two dreamers had to say about the human spirit and our quest for answers, I'm ready to volunteer for the next NASA space mission.

Some people object to the cost of the space program, believing that the tax money would be better spent on programs that target problems much closer to home than the stars. It is not a bad point but, in a way, the space program has paid for itself in the technological advances that affect our everyday lives, which NASA's research and testing has generated. The space program has developed more than thirty thousand techniques and products, from lightweight, high-strength plastic piping to fireproofing materials; from modular housing to techniques that increase the shelf life of food.

There is another extremely good reason why we should be

shooting for the stars, and it is one that Carl Sagan suggested may be the best reason of all: "By exploring other worlds we safeguard this one."

That statement can be taken many ways, but I take it as cautionary, even a warning, that what we learn from exploring other worlds may tell us a great deal about our own—about our past, our present, and the future. And it will prepare us psychologically and technologically for what may be the most dangerous moment that humans have ever faced: *first contact.*

So far we have never set human foot on another planet. Despite the robotic mini laboratories we have sent, we don't know exactly what type of extraterrestrial life is in our own solar system.

For our own protection and peace of mind, we should know what is happening with our nearest neighbors—including planet-killing asteroids we need to find and neutralize.

Let's take a look at the evidence that proves we are not alone.

42

Exoplanets.

The most significant reason scientists now assume there is life beyond Earth is the discovery of exoplanets that could support life as we know it.

An exoplanet, also called an extrasolar planet, is a planet orbiting a star other than our sun. An exoplanet is of particular interest in the search for life if its orbit is in what would be considered the "habitable zone" of the star's solar system.

The habitable zone is usually defined as the area in which liquid water can exist on the surface—in other words, a region not so hot that water boils away or so cold that it is always frozen. Life as we know it requires liquid water, though not necessarily conditions amenable to humans. Forms of "life" on our planet have been found in boiling cauldrons miles deep in our oceans, under ice shelves millions of years old, and in baths of acid.

We pretty much assume that "life" is restricted to biological entities. Whether there are forms of existence that we don't think of as life as we know it is a different issue, and certainly needs to be addressed by science.

Many other factors would be considered germane in evaluating an exoplanet's ability to support life, but as simple as it sounds, a presumption that the most probable place to find life outside our solar system is on an exoplanet whose orbit is in its star's habitable zone has tremendous logic. Obviously, if a planet is too hot, too cold, or too gaseous, we can eliminate it. And once the availability of water is found, scientists must make sure the planet has other sustaining factors, such as biochemical compounds and an energy source, which create an invitation for life to erupt.

I won't bore you with the math, but although only a couple thousand exoplanets have actually been discovered, it's estimated that the number of extrasolar planets in habitable zones in our Milky Way galaxy number in the tens of billions.

The notion that life can exist only in the well-defined habitable zone where liquid water is available is being challenged by the fact that even outside the defined habitable zone, planetary energy sources could create an environment for liquid water—a subterranean sea, for example. There also is scientific dispute over what would be too hot or too cold for life-forms, and over the idea that there may be forms of life that are not dependent on liquid water.

But, in terms of answering the question about whether we are alone in the universe, adding in alternative theories of life based on factors not in our own chemistry merely opens even wider the door to finding life on other planets, literally adding to the list tens of billions of potential exoplanets where life in one form or another could exist.

If we look past the Milky Way to other galaxies, the billions would become trillions.

When we start dealing with such incredible numbers, the notion that we are alone in the universe is hard for me to accept.

LIFE SPREADING ACROSS THE UNIVERSE LIKE AN EPIDEMIC

Some scientists believe there are two ways that life, even intelligent life, can spread across the universe: through intentional travel and through biological transfer via comets and asteroids.

There is a theory that the first primordial life came to Earth via an asteroid or comet, perhaps along with vast amounts of water that created our oceans. The theory is called panspermia.

Astrophysicists at the Harvard–Smithsonian Center for Astrophysics also theorize that, if panspermia occurred, life could spread out in pockets, "seeding" planets that can sustain life, such as those in the habitable zone. This can be thought of as spreading life as bacteria or a virus spreads, "infecting" planets that are capable of sustaining life.

43

Moons of life.

We may not have to look beyond our own solar system to find extraterrestrial life. It may be within reach in our own solar system, where the habitable zone gets stretched to let in some candidates that, for one reason or another, have the right conditions.

Temperatures on Mars, for example, create a tolerance for liquid water in a number of regions during some times of the year. It also has been established that Mars was once a "wet" planet with lakes and rivers.

A bit farther away, Saturn's icy moon Enceladus is shooting long sheets of water out from its surface of clean ice. Studies reveal that Enceladus not only has water but also has two other key ingredients necessary for life: organic chemicals and an energy source in a six-mile-deep ocean. Jupiter's moons Europa and Ganymede also have oceans trapped under ice, with Europa also shooting out water vapor plumes and, like Enceladus, showing evidence of organic materials.

And again, we don't want to eliminate the potential for forms of life not similar to our own. Saturn's moon Titan, for example, has low levels of oxygen and lakes of liquid methane. Humans would not be able to survive on Titan, though methane-based life-forms could. We have sea mussels here on Earth, living in deep oceanic methane seeps, that actually use bacteria in their gills to turn methane gas into energy.

One obvious change we need to make in our current approach to finding life beyond our planet is to stop looking just for the elements that make life possible on Earth. As with exoplanets, we need to determine what other forms of life can exist on moons (and planets) with atmospheres too extreme for life as we know it to exist. If, eons ago, Mars or the moons of Saturn or Jupiter had life-forms that are now, or always have been, beneath the surface and thus able to withstand the extremes of temperature on the surface, it may be well advanced beyond our own level of intelligence and technology.

44

God and aliens.

Is there a conflict between the concept of God and the presence of life on other planets?

I suppose the simple answer is that, if there is an omnipotent deity, then by definition God could create both us terrestrials and extraterrestrials. Likewise, the discovery of life on other planets would neither prove nor disprove the existence of God.

This view is promulgated by the largest Christian church on the planet, with more a billion members: the Roman Catholic Church. The Church is also religiously conservative and would hardly take a position about life on other planets that would conflict with its views of God and the universe.

My own view is that there should not be a conflict between science and religion, that both fields enrich our lives and each can act as a balance for the other.

I do give credit to the Church of Rome for calling attention to and examining the potential conflict between religious beliefs and the potential presence of life throughout the universe. The Church has an astronomical research facility, the Vatican Observatory, in the Alban Hills at Castel Gandolfo, a town about fifteen miles southeast of Rome. It also has a facility at the Mount Graham International Observatory in Arizona's Pinaleño Mountains. The Church's astronomy staff has conducted studies and hosted conferences that include individuals from scientific fields (astronomy, biology, astrophysics, and physics) to discuss the existence of extraterrestrial life.

Although the Catholic Church, with its observatory and

astronomical studies, seems to have been the most verbal and active about extraterrestrial life, interest in the possible existence of extraterrestrials has been sparked among many religious groups by the discovery of exoplanets and the realization that we soon will be able to detect whether the components of "life" exist on one or more of them.

I rather like Pope Francis's description of how he would handle the situation if little green men from Mars showed up at his doorstep: he would baptize them.

This, of course, from a pope whose predecessor, nearly four hundred years ago, persecuted Galileo for looking through his telescope. And before Galileo was silenced in 1633 for stating that Earth revolves around the sun, Giordano Bruno, a Dominican friar in Italy, was burned at the stake in 1600 for proposing that the stars are actually suns with their own planets, which might contain life. Friar Bruno also stated that the universe is infinite and that there is no celestial body at its center. He was able to look up at the infinite sky and see beyond what others saw.

He endured a horrible death from those with closed minds, for seeing the truth and speaking it.

I'd like to think that the world today is far beyond such mindless brutality against science and free thinking, but looking at the horrors committed by terrorist groups in the Middle East and Afghanistan invokes images of the ignorance and atrocities of the Dark Ages and medieval times.

That the discovery of extraterrestrial life is probably years—not decades—away should add some urgency to how religious groups will deal with the subject.

45

Microbes or giants.

What kind of life is "out there"? Microbes or giants? Bacteria or apes? Animal, mineral, or vegetable? Big flesh-ripping teeth and claws or something of unimaginable beauty and grace?

Do they have the same chemistry as us or as other forms of life on our planet, or a totally different biochemistry? Perhaps there is a form of "life" that we would not even recognize or consider to be a life-form? Something inorganic, like a rock?

Would we even be able to recognize their existence, if we are looking for a life-form with traits that exist on Earth?

The most important trait, whether it is like ours or has some other basis, is intelligence. An apelike creature that thinks we belong in a zoo would be infinitely more interesting than a bacteria we can only see under a microscope.

Speaking of intelligence, another life-form may well wonder whether there is intelligent life on Earth, once it takes a look at our history. Surely there has never been a single day on our planet, during recorded history, that a significant number of people haven't died from war or other violence.

We are reaching for the stars, but there are still parts of our world that are culturally in the Dark Ages, despite the widespread use of cars, planes, television, smartphones, and the Internet in those regions.

Walter Sullivan, in *We Are Not Alone*, asked whether we are smart enough to suppress our aggressions and prejudices in order to survive the crises that confront us in our world. And he pointed out that if we lack that ability, chances are that extraterrestrials also will lack it.

Most movies about extraterrestrials portray them as hideous creatures and monsters, and those images are imprinted in our psyches. Will first contact create a reaction in us similar to the panic that gripped some people in 1938 with the Orson Welles broadcast of a dramatization of H. G. Wells's 1898 novel *The War of the Worlds*? A *shoot first and ask questions later* reaction?

I hope there is enough intelligent life on our planet that, when that first contact occurs, we have a plan of action in place to deal with the situation in a manner that protects our security in case of attack while leaving us open to welcome the new arrivals as guests if they are peaceful.

I would bet that no such plan exists. Even if the United States had such a plan, there are plenty of nations that would shoot first.

We are technologically intelligent human beings, reaching out to the stars, but we live in a world where too many people can't see beyond their indefensible prejudices and murderous passions.

46

Stone Age weapons versus planet-killing devices?

We have no idea who—or what—is out there, other than that they are most assuredly out there and someday we will meet them.

If they get to us before we get to them, it is a sure bet that they will be technologically vastly superior to us. That is especially true if they come from outside our solar system, because the nearest star to us is Proxima Centauri, which is 4.2 light-years away. That means it takes more than four years for light, which travels at 186,000 miles per second (671 million miles per hour), to get there. According to NASA, our *Voyager* spacecraft left the solar system at 37,000 miles per hour. At that speed, it would take it eighty thousand years to reach Proxima Centauri.

If we are going to get visitors from the stars, they obviously would need to be far more technologically advanced than we are. And we aren't going to be visiting any star systems until we solve some of the technical problems that keep us from going faster than we currently can.

My understanding of the big bang theory is that the universe came into being nearly fourteen billion years ago through a fiery explosion, expansion, whatever you want to call it, sending out matter that ultimately formed planets, stars, and whatever else we have in the universe. According to this theory, matter closest to the expansion would have coalesced before matter shot farther out.

If the big bang theory is correct, then it's pretty certain that extraterrestrials nearer than us to the core of the big bang are far advanced, in terms of technology. Our planet was formed less than five billion years ago, which means there may be planets that are billions of years older. That's *billions of years* to develop technology more advanced than ours. However, looking at it from another viewpoint, it took us nearly five billion years to get to this point and we haven't gotten a person farther than the moon.

Going back to basics, we can pretty well anticipate that whoever shows up at our planet's doorstep, from wherever, will be far advanced compared to us because they got here first. That means we could be facing weapons capable of destroying planets, like the Death Star in *Star Wars*, while even our nuclear weapons are Stone Age in comparison.

They might consider us to be children or imbeciles—or they might take one look at our world and see so much mindless war and violence that they run away, frightened of whatever virus might be causing our lack of humanity toward each other.

47

Message in a bottle, cast into the galactic sea.

The *Pioneer* and *Voyager* spacecraft carried messages aboard to introduce ourselves to any extraterrestrials who stumble upon them.

Pioneer 10 and *Pioneer 11* (launched in 1972 and 1973) each carried a six-by-nine-inch gold-anodized aluminum plaque. The plaques feature a drawing of the nude figures of a man and a woman, along with several symbols that provide information about where the spacecraft came from.

Voyager 1 and *Voyager 2*, launched in 1977, each contained a Voyager Golden Record, which are twelve-inch copper-plated phonograph records with sounds and images that portray life and culture on Earth.

The late Carl Sagan was involved in the planning and implementation of both the *Pioneer* and *Voyager* messages. He said that the spacecraft will be encountered and the record played only if there are advanced space-faring civilizations in interstellar space. Launching the record was the equivalent of tossing a "bottle into the cosmic ocean."

At the time of this writing, *Voyager 1* has journeyed farther from Earth than any man-made object; it has left the solar system but is still many thousands of years from the nearest star in the direction it is going.

Some people have been alarmed that we have sent spacecraft containing messages into space. The concern is not only that it lets someone or something "out there" know how to find us but also that the space vehicle itself carries messages that reveal the level of our technology. Knowledge of that level of technical achievement would reveal the probable nature of our weaponry.

Of course, we have been sending radio waves at the speed of light into space for more than a hundred years, ever since radio pioneer Guglielmo Marconi and others started sending "wireless telegraph," followed by radio and television.

It may be that, as I write this, a little green person on Proxima Centauri is having a belly laugh as they watch Lucy and Ethel shove chocolates into their mouths as the conveyor belt speeds up.

What the little green person would think about the graphic violence in our films and our news reports isn't a laughing matter.

I seriously doubt that there is any danger from an alien finding our message in a bottle and coming back to us, even though that was the premise of John Carpenter's *Starman* film.

Just as we are learning about other worlds through deep space telescopic probes, I think it's probable that someone—or something—out there is looking at us right now.

Besides sending *I Love Lucy*, *The X-Files*, *Baywatch*, and a vast amount of entertainment, news, and whatever into space for decades, Stephen Hawking, the British cosmologist, and Yuri Milner, a Russian Silicon Valley billionaire, launched a $100 million project to search for extraterrestrial life in the universe. It's called the Breakthrough Listen project and it will have some of the largest telescopes on the planet search deep into space for artificial radio or laser signals. The project is associated with Milner's Breakthrough Message, a project to devise a suitable message that can then be sent out from Earth to let extraterrestrials know we are here.

Sending out signals will obviously cover vastly more territory than a spacecraft carrying a physical message. And it stimulates more issues about whether we should be letting anyone know we are here.

Based upon her studies of different cultures, Margaret Mead, the great anthropologist, made the observation that we should not respond to an attempt by an extraterrestrial civilization to contact us because it is always disastrous for a technologically inferior civilization to meet a superior one.

48

Is this the one?

Occasionally, a planet discovered by Kepler, a space observatory launched by NASA in 2009 to discover Earthlike planets orbiting other stars, gets NASA excited. One, designated Kepler-452b, grabbed NASA's attention because of its exoplanet stats: Kepler-452b lies in the habitable zone of a G2 star and takes 385 days to orbit the star.

Translating those facts to our own terms, our own sun, Old Man Sol, is also a G2 star, so Kepler-452b's sun has a temperature and density similar to that of Sol. In fact, scientists believe that, viewed from Kepler-452b, its G2 sun would look pretty similar to how our own sun looks to us.

Scientists estimate that the exoplanet is larger than Earth and thus has more mass and more surface gravity. Because the G2 star is about six billion years old, whereas Sol is about four and a half billion years old, the exoplanet may get about 10 percent more heat from its sun than we do from ours. That would make Kepler-452b warmer than Earth and perhaps would even have created a runaway greenhouse effect of heat and atmospheric moisture. The planet may be covered with thick, misty clouds.

Because of its mass, it likely has many active volcanoes.

Kepler-452b is about 1,400 light-years away, meaning that light sent from Earth at about the time the Roman Empire was crashing and burning (around AD 500) would just be arriving in that solar system. Fourteen hundred light-years away also means we are not going to be heading out for it anytime soon. But that doesn't mean that the exoplanet doesn't have life far more advanced than ours, or that these beings haven't visited us. Could Kepler-452b travelers be the ones behind our ancient and modern extraterrestrial sightings?

Since the exoplanet has been around a billion and a half years longer than Mother Earth, it has had the opportunity to be eons ahead of us in terms of technology.

It took four and a half billion years for *Homo sapiens* to get to the moon, but after that breakthrough, one has to imagine that in another million—or billion—years we will have a good handle on even intergalactic travel.

Life on Kepler-452b may well have developed eons earlier than we did on Earth, or much later. No one knows. But the possibility is there, because it matches up so well with our own environment.

There is also another possibility: that the miracle of creation never took place at all on the planet.

But if not there, then somewhere else, perhaps even on closer cousin Kepler-438b, which is in the constellation Lyra, a mere 470 light-years away. Kepler-438b even has a slightly better Earth Similarity Index score.

It really doesn't matter whether either Kepler is "the one." There are plenty more exoplanets in the habitable zone, and we will hit the jackpot someday. Unlike what you find in Vegas, the odds are heavily in favor of us having company in the universe.

My father during WWII.

My mom, Fitchburg,
Massachusetts, 1948.

My parents, August 20, 1949.

My father, his twin brother,
my grandparents, and cousins.

The "Five G's" 1950s.

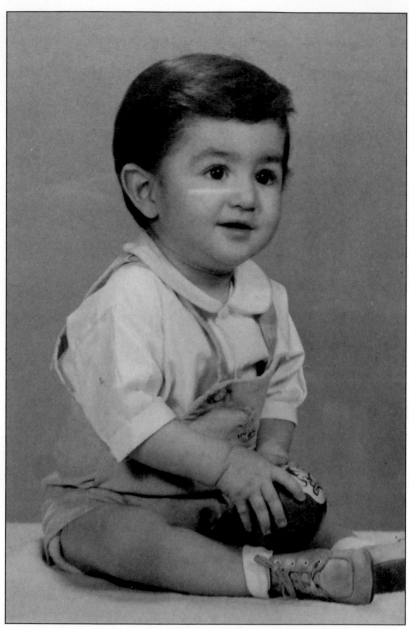

Me with sideburns.

At 18—with sideburns.

My parents, 2011.

With my sisters,
Glinda and Gail.

My grandchildren.

Being awarded the Michigan Associated Press Broadcasting Association General Excellence Award by Michigan governor William Milliken, 1977.

All in a day's work!

PART VIII

WHERE IS EVERYONE?

If there are extraterrestrials, why aren't they here?

A Nobel Prize–winning scientist asked this question, which became known as the Fermi paradox.

Let's take a look at the scientist and his question, and then I will tell you the answer.

49

Back in 1950, physicist Enrico Fermi questioned why, if there are billions of stars in the universe, with billions of planets capable of producing life, we haven't been visited by extraterrestrials.

Referred to as the Fermi paradox (or the Fermi-Hart paradox, to include a scientist who enlarged upon the subject), the topic is more complex than I want to go into, but I want to respond to Fermi's basic question about why, it appears, we haven't been visited by extraterrestrials.

Fermi was a Nobel Prize–winning, world-renowned physicist who is included among those called "father of the atomic bomb." Bearing that in mind, I believe that what I see as his premise—that, because billions of years have passed, spacecraft should be buzzing around the universe—assumes too much.

Fermi made the statement in 1950, just three years after test pilot Chuck Yeager broke the sound barrier, in 1947. Yeager's feat was accomplished by flying a plane 805 miles per hour, a little over the 767 miles per hour needed to break the barrier.

Thus, after nearly five billion years, a life-form on our planet managed to fly faster than the 767 miles per hour at which sound travels.

That leaves us rather short of managing the speed of light (671 million miles per hour) that would enable us to reach even the nearest star, which is about four light-years away. And there are stars that are billions of light-years away.

We are still far from the technology invented by Hollywood,

where Han Solo or Captain Kirk snaps his fingers to cross galaxies at warp speed.

Considering the distance and how long it has taken us just to get up to "sound speed," I don't believe we should expect our skies to be crowded with alien spaceships. However, considering all that, plus the fact there are most probably extraterrestrial civilizations far more advanced than us, maybe millions or even billions of years further advanced, I also don't believe it is unlikely that one or more alien civilizations is capable of reaching us.

However, my answer to Fermi's question is really quite simple.

If you look at the evidence, it clearly shows that *they are already here*!

50

They are here.

How do I know they're here? I've looked at the evidence.

Who are these "extraterrestrials," these ETs about whom we joke about phoning home and loosely refer to as "aliens"? Raging monsters it takes a Sigourney Weaver to stomp? Naked guys like Jeff Bridges in *Starman*? Mysterious, philosophical shape-changers similar to those Carl Sagan created in *Contact*?

It's a certainty that whatever mental image each of us has of extraterrestrials, the image has been influenced by books and movies.

On a basic level, extraterrestrials are simply a life-form not of this planet. Maybe they look just like us. Or perhaps they are shaped differently but with a chemistry we would recognize as similar to ours. Or maybe they are something that has no relation to or appearance like us humans. An entity so different from man, beast, bug, or microbe that we don't even recognize it as a life-form.

There is one certainty, which I have mentioned before: if they made it *here* before we made it *there*, it is highly probable that they are far more technologically advanced than we are.

Another fact appears evident: they don't need to have journeyed here from "a galaxy far, far away," as we are told in the *Star Wars* opening crawl titles. The closest exoplanet is buzzing around a star a little over four light-years away. That's quite a hop but, as we know, there is no reason to doubt that there are extraterrestrials that are thousands or even millions of years ahead of us technologically. Or they live much closer than we suspect, maybe on the very planet we will be landing on next: Mars.

With more evidence popping up about water on Mars, plus those other planets' moons we discussed that are candidates for hosting life, the toll charge for ET to call home may be less than we have imagined—perhaps "home" is within our own solar system.

As I mentioned earlier, my first fascination with aliens didn't come from comic books or a television show about Buck Rogers, Flash Gordon, or space cadets but from *We Are Not Alone*, by *New York Times* science journalist Walter Sullivan. Sullivan's premise was an exciting and tantalizing thought—even more so back then than it is today, when the idea of life somewhere else in the universe is becoming more accepted.

But Sullivan wrote about extraterrestrials somewhere far away, not next door, in the next town or state. But if we accept the premises of Sullivan, Carl Sagan, and many others that there is life on other planets, there is a high possibility that some of it has gotten here.

That is especially true when we consider those studies I mentioned earlier, which indicate that there are billions of stars just in our Milky Way galaxy that can support planets capable of producing life, and the fact that some of those exoplanets are billions of years older and thus probably much more advanced.

Taking into consideration those factors that would support the existence of life on other planets, life that may in fact be far more advanced technologically than we are, in turn supports a conclusion that there is no reason to assume that aliens are physically unable reach us.

In addition to the fact that it is possible for extraterrestrials to reach us, there is a great deal of evidence that we have been visited—even "invaded" and "occupied," perhaps going back thousands of years.

I have appeared a number of times on the History Channel's

Ancient Aliens series, in which historical texts, legends, and artifacts are examined to see whether they contain evidence of visitations to Earth by extraterrestrials over the millennia.

My conclusions are that aliens not only were present in ancient times but also are present today, that the existence of aliens on Earth is deliberately being kept secret by the government, and that extraterrestrials have the ability to exert control over our government.

Sound like a conspiracy theory? Or an episode of a History Channel show I have been a guest on? Or an episode of *Beyond Belief*?

It sounds like many things, but these also are conclusions that I have reached after years of investigation. And I do not jump to conclusions. I search for the truth. I want to see evidence.

51

When I speak about evidence of extraterrestrial visitations, I am not talking about beyond-a-shadow-of-a-doubt evidence that lawyers and judges jaw over—and over—and over. That kind of evidence is tempered by court rules that often exclude valuable testimony.

If an alien spaceship flopped down in Times Square and a little green person popped out, things would be simple . . . though as I write these words I realize that if that happened in Times Square, people would just think it was a stunt to advertise a new smartphone—one the size of a wedding band, or even a nose ring, the way things are going.

Joking aside, a terrible problem surrounding discussion of extraterrestrials on or visiting our planet is the ridicule and derision that the subject brings up. And, as the late Carl Sagan pointed out, people are polarized about the subject. People tend either to ignore evidence of sightings or to conclude, without evidence, that extraterrestrials are here and are in control, because some people eagerly accept UFO incidents as real even in the face of meager evidence, while others reject the notion of aliens out of hand because they don't want it to be true.

Sagan believed both attitudes get in the way of serious study of a phenomenon reported by thousands of people around the world.

There is little physical evidence that points directly at an extraterrestrial presence on Earth. There are some photos that appear to be authentic, but there also have been many dumb jokes played, in which people created phony photos as a joke.

Most of the evidence is provided by eyewitnesses. Sometimes a UFO is spotted by a single individual, with no corroboration from other sources. That does not make the sighting false. It simply makes it harder to prove, because others will be quick to argue that there is no proof—ignoring the fact that a fellow human being is reporting the sighting.

If we could not rely upon the testimony of a single eyewitness, our criminal justice system would collapse. Indeed, the legal system is based not only on eyewitnesses but also on circumstantial evidence, in which no one actually saw the culprit commit the crime yet pieces of evidence are linked together until they end up at the perpetrator's door.

We have to look at the circumstances of a UFO sighting, the conditions under which the sighting occurred, and the credibility of the person reporting the sighting.

Credibility is usually the most important factor. That means we look at the witness's background, whether they have reported other events, the circumstances and physical conditions surrounding the sightings, and whether their observations are consistent with what other people at other times and places have reported. In other words, is this a person we would trust to make a truthful and accurate report or someone who appears to be unreliable?

Fortunately for those of us who give some credence to UFO sightings and the presence of extraterrestrials on our soil, there have been a large number of credible sightings not just by an individual alone but even by large groups of people, all seeing the same thing at the same time.

The downside of eyewitness accounts of extraterrestrial activity is that it doesn't matter how many witnesses there are or how credible they are, the sightings are repeatedly ignored or discounted by government authorities. Ignored and discounted in the rare event that the authorities have even investigated the reports.

Most often the reports are simply ignored and no investigation is done to corroborate or otherwise categorize the sighting. When faced with determined people who won't accept denial that they saw something, the next line of government denial is that the event either was unusual weather or was a weather balloon, which is how the authorities characterized the Roswell incident—a lie that took decades to unravel.

As we go through the reports from the past decades, what stands out as absolutely stunning, even bizarre, is the number of UFO sightings that have been discounted or ignored even though the reports came from the most credible possible sources: commercial airline pilots, military pilots, even air force reconnaissance crews—individuals who have been highly trained as observers.

Some of the most astonishing reports were treated as if the very credible people making the reports were hallucinating.

We'll start with startling facts about sightings in ancient times.

Of all government agencies to get involved in investigating UFO and extraterrestrial sighting from thousands of years ago, one would think that NASA would be last on the list. Yet most of the sightings from ancient times I discuss here are drawn from a NASA report on UFOs.

52

In 2007, the National Aeronautics and Space Administration's Goddard Institute for Space Studies published a report outlining sightings of UFOs during the time of the Roman Empire.

Entitled *Unidentified Flying Objects in Classical Antiquity*, the sightings were drawn from Roman-era chronicles. The summary at the beginning of the report notes that, after eliminating "conventionally explicable phenomena" (such as clouds, for example), there still are "puzzling reports" of UFOs during these ancient times. The abstract describing the report reads:

A combined historical and scientific approach is applied to ancient reports of what might today be called unidentified flying objects (UFOs). Many conventionally explicable phenomena can be weeded out, leaving a small residue of puzzling reports. These fall neatly into the same categories as modern UFO reports, suggesting that the UFO phenomenon, whatever it may be due to, has not changed much over two millennia.

The noteworthy events are spread over several centuries, starting in 218 BC, when "a spectacle of ships (*navium*) gleamed in the sky."

The next year "at Arpi round shields (*parmas*) were seen in the sky." Observations of "shields" in the sky were made a number of times, as were observations of fleets of ships.

The most famous incident described in the report was recorded by the historian Josephus. It occurred in AD 65 over what is now modern Israel and was then a Roman province. Josephus was a first-century Jewish scholar, historian, and military leader who was born in Jerusalem and grew up to lead a Jewish army in an unsuccessful revolt against the Romans in the year 66.

Josephus reported that, during the year prior to the revolt, a "sky army" or "sky battle" occurred. This is how the event is related in the NASA report:

> On the 21st of the month Artemisium, there appeared a miraculous phenomenon, passing belief. Indeed, what I am about to relate would, I imagine, have been deemed a fable, were it not for the narratives of eyewitnesses and the subsequent calamities which deserved to be so signalized. For, before sunset throughout all parts of the country, chariots were seen in the air and armed battalions hurtling through the clouds and encompassing the cities.

The NASA report notes, "The phenomenon does not seem to have been an aurora, cloud patterns or meteors, but does resemble the 'aerial fighting' of modern UFOs."

The report also states, in its Conclusions section, that the events related were "culled" from a larger number:

> This collection of what might be termed ancient UFO reports has been culled from a much larger number of reports of aerial objects, most of whose identifications with known phenomena are either certain or at least highly probable. Embedded in the mass of relatively explicable ancient reports, however, is a small set of unexplained (or at least not wholly explained) reports from presumably credible witnesses.

The report is signed "Richard Stothers, National Aeronautics and Space Administration." I like Mr. Stothers's concluding remarks about the fact that UFO sightings have been persistently with us over the millennia:

> Whether one prefers to think in terms of universal recurrent visions from the collective unconscious, misperceptions of ordinary objects, unusual atmospheric effects, unknown physical phenomena or extraterrestrial visitations, what we today would call UFOs possess an intrinsic interest that has transcended the passage of time and the increase of human knowledge.

53

Not included in the NASA report is an event that occurred before Roman times, when Alexander the Great is said to have observed two "shields" spitting fire in the sky while his army was at a river crossing. Other UFO "sky battles" also are not mentioned in the report because they didn't occur in antiquity. I find several that occurred during the Renaissance to be of interest because they were mass sightings in which thousands of people were eyewitnesses. Adding a bit to the credibility, they also occurred not in isolated rural areas but over prominent cities and thus would have been observable by people with scientific backgrounds.

Another very prominent event occurred in Nuremburg, Germany. Nuremburg was the center of what has been called the German Renaissance, because of its emphasis on classical reasoning, the arts, literature, politics, and the natural sciences during the general Renaissance, which began in Italy and spread throughout Europe during the fourteenth to seventeenth centuries. Given the city's cultural background, we can infer that a great many of its citizens were sophisticated in terms of understanding natural phenomena, such as cloud formations and other atmospheric disturbances, that can appear to be strange objects.

The sighting occurred the morning of April 14, 1561, when round and rod-shaped objects appeared to battle in the sky overhead.

Five years later, there was a similar sighting in Basel, Switzerland.

More round objects were observed in 1697, over Hamburg, Germany, which like Nuremburg and Basel, is a major city. Again, the objects were round—in this case, described as wheel-shaped.

Another interesting sighting occurred in 1609, in China, when, on a clear, cloudless day, a shiny bowl-shaped object flew across the sky and made a thunderous sound that shook the earth.

Sound like a flying object breaking the sound barrier?

UFO skeptics often claim that the "flying saucer" shape of many modern unidentified flying object sightings was inspired by people watching science fiction movies. But it's obvious that round UFOs, often described as shield-shaped, have been recorded since the time of Alexander the Great and the Romans.

The saucer shape not only goes back thousands of years but also, like UFOs in general, has been persistently reported over the millennia—right up to modern times, and *the invasion of Earth by extraterrestrials.*

54

"Invasion" is a strong word to use about a subject as hotly debated as extraterrestrials.

I called the flood of UFO sightings that began in the 1940s an "invasion" in my novel *Night Talk*. That was a work of fiction, of course, but the references to extraterrestrial incidents in the book were for the most part based upon events reported by people in different parts of the world.

When it comes to the eyewitness accounts about extraterrestrials, as with so many things in our world, truth can be stranger than fiction.

To understand the invasion, we need to take a step back some decades, to the forties and the Second World War.

We'll start with a shooting barrage that some ufologists consider an extraterrestrial incident but which others scoff at and dismiss as a weather balloon igniting a case of war nerves. It's called the Battle of Los Angeles or the Great Los Angeles Air Raid. Both names are used facetiously.

In early 1942, less than three months after the attack on Pearl Harbor, a Japanese submarine surfaced near the Ellwood Oil Field near Santa Barbara, California, and fired at the installation. Although the sub fired up to a couple dozen artillery rounds, only minor damage occurred. However, the attack did send jitters about a Japanese invasion throughout the West Coast and the country as a whole.

The next evening, in Los Angeles, searchlights swept the sky and, when something was spotted, military gunners began firing machine guns, flares, and antiaircraft rounds that burst in the night, creating a barrage.

That was the Battle of Los Angeles.

This is what triggered me to join ufologists in questioning the official cause of the incident: forty-one years later, the U.S. Office of Air Force History listed the cause of the incident as a case of war nerves, probably triggered by a *weather balloon.* Attribution of the case to a weather balloon is what causes my eyes to roll. As I have mentioned, clouds and weather balloons are how most UFO incidents are "explained" by the government, including at Roswell, where it took the government nearly fifty years to admit that it wasn't a weather balloon.

At the time, prompted by newspaper accusations of a cover-up and demands for answers, the War Department (today's Department of Defense) held hearings about the incident. At the conclusion of the fact taking, the Secretary of War (today's Secretary of Defense) announced that the incident was caused by unidentified aircraft flying over the city. It was assumed that the aircraft had been under Japanese control.

After the war, the Japanese government revealed that it had no aircraft involved in the incident.

The fact that official word at the highest level, after an investigation, concluded that the incident was ignited by flying objects in the sky did not bother the air force at all, forty-one years later, when it reviewed the evidence.

The air force looked at the evidence and realized that our aircraft couldn't have been flying over, because we knew we didn't have any up there, and it couldn't have been Japanese aircraft because they didn't have any up there, either.

Faced with the fact that the air force had to come up with a flying object, anyway, I imagine someone took a pencil and drew a line through the word "aircraft" and scribbled above it "weather balloon."

55

There is another World War II UFO incident, and it involved two men who would make anyone's list of the greatest leaders of the twentieth century. But first I want to tell you a little about foo fighters—not the rock band but an aerial phenomenon from the war.

Of the two great leaders I mentioned, one has a connection to the foo fighters: General Dwight D. Eisenhower, thirty-fourth president of the United States.

"Foo fighter" is a term borrowed from a comic strip. It was used during World War II to describe mysterious UFOs sightings by fighter pilots and aircrews in both Europe and the Pacific. The objects were described as round, fast-moving, fiery objects that glowed red, white, or orange and appeared to fly in formation. Pilots and crewmen described the UFOs as seeming to be under control, but they would play or toy with aircraft they were following. Attempts to outmaneuver them or shoot them down failed. They came and went as they liked and never displayed hostile intentions, other than their presence.

In the European Theater of Operations they were first seen over Germany and were thought to be a German secret weapon. In December 1944, Supreme Headquarters, Allied Expeditionary Force, under the command of General Eisenhower, issued a statement that described the phenomenon as a new German weapon. However, with the defeat of Germany and Japan and access to the war records and military personnel of the defeated nations, it was discovered that both German and Japanese pilots had made similar sightings.

The fact that General Eisenhower's command had designated foo fighters as aircraft didn't bother the revisionists at all. In 1953, eight years after the war, the Robertson Panel, a government advisory group created on the recommendation of the CIA, decided the phenomenon was probably electromagnetic, electrostatic, or just reflections of light from ice crystals.

The fact that witnesses were experienced pilots and aircrew, who had seen clouds and other weather phenomena hundreds of times, didn't matter to the revisionists.

56

Back in the Old West, in the days of cattle drives and gunslingers, the highest compliment a cowboy could pay another cowboy was to say, "He's a man to ride the river with."

"Riding the river" referred to driving a herd of cattle across a river. It was a dangerous part of a cattle drive and could get especially treacherous when it was done at night. When the horses and cattle got into the water, their footing became unstable and they could easily panic and become unmanageable. When that happened, the horse could go down and its rider could drown.

Two men who I would have liked to have ridden the river with were Prime Minister Winston Churchill and General Eisenhower.

It just happens that they have a connection to the most provocative UFO sighting of the Second World War.

D-day, the invasion of Normandy, came off on June 6, 1944. After getting their footing on the beaches, the Allies fought their way to Paris and liberated the city with the help of the French Resistance, then headed for the Rhine.

In August, the crew of a Royal Air Force reconnaissance plane returning home over the English Channel after a mission reported that a strange aircraft, nothing that they were familiar with, had intercepted their plane. It hovered near them, maintaining speed and distance, then flew off at high speed.

A report of the incident states that Churchill, Eisenhower, and their intelligence chiefs met and discussed the encounter.

The net result was that the incident was declared top secret. People were already war weary and shouldn't have to worry about a strange entity that could be a new enemy.

When I relate this story in my novel, the female protagonist asks, "What sort of corroboration is there of the sighting?"

That's a good question. After all this time, how do we know that this Royal Air Force reconnaissance plane actually had a strange encounter with an unidentified flying object?

The male protagonist in the novel makes this reply:

> "The incident was revealed sixty-six years later in 2010 by the BBC after the United Kingdom's National Archives released the information. While pilots in general are in a good position to judge other flying objects, it's interesting that it was the crew of a military reconnaissance plane that made the report. We have to assume that these wartime airmen were highly trained observers whose job it was to report accurately what they saw."

Although the character is fiction, the information in the reply is not.

Isn't it amazing? Buried for more than six decades in Britain's National Archive is an incident involving extraterrestrials and two of the greatest leaders of the twentieth century.

It brings to mind the scene at the end of *Raiders of the Lost Ark*, where the most powerful object known to mankind is casually placed in an overcrowded warehouse that smacks of bureaucratic inattention.

The point about the report being made by airmen of a reconnaissance mission is especially significant. It has to be presumed that, among those brave warriors who fought in the war, men trained and experienced in reconnaissance would report an incident accurately—more precisely and in more detail than those not trained in wartime aerial observation. And, because so many lives depended on their observations, their reports would seem to carry the greatest weight.

It appears that the cover-up began to unravel and ultimately was exposed when an individual attempted to find out more information about an incident in which his grandfather, who served in the Royal Air Force during the Second World War, had attended a meeting in which Churchill and Eisenhower discussed how to deal with the UFO encounter. The reconnaissance plane incident is part of five thousand pages of UFO documents released from the archives in 2010.

I can't walk away from this subject without mentioning that there is one more provocative aspect to this incident that involves giants of history and an unanswered question.

The plane's crew reported that they had photographed the object as it hovered near them.

Where are the photographs?

57

A reasonable person should be shocked, as we go through the "invasion" scenarios, about the obviously credible sightings rejected by the authorities after no investigation, a bungled investigation, or even a deliberate cover-up. The sightings get disregarded by the authorities, despite the status and experience of the people reporting them.

In the case I am about to describe, there were even independent eyewitness confirmations of the sighting. It involves an individual named Kenneth Arnold.

Arnold was both a pilot active in search and rescue operations and a successful businessman in Idaho. In June 1947, Arnold was flying his plane near Mount Rainer in Washington State, a stunning volcanic peak that rises more than fourteen thousand feet. At the time, he was on the lookout for a military transport plane that reportedly had crashed in the area. Instead of the wreck, he observed nine saucerlike UFOs flying in formation at speeds faster than aircraft of that day could achieve.

Arnold reported the sighting and the military conducted an investigation, which labeled the observation an optical illusion, despite Arnold's status as an experienced pilot and observer involved in search and rescue missions. And it ignored an eyewitness account in addition to Arnold's.

A man on the ground, a prospector, reported that he had seen six of the UFOs with the use of a small telescope. A separate set of investigators interviewed the prospector and reported that the prospector was credible.

The experienced pilot in the air with the UFOs was found to be not credible. The prospector was found to be credible. And both were reporting the same incident.

A total of sixteen sightings were reported in the same region, and a turn of the screw came shortly thereafter.

On July 4, ten days after the reported sighting, the pilot and copilot of an airliner flying over Idaho on its way to Seattle, Washington, reported that a UFO similar to what Arnold had described had paced their plane for ten to fifteen minutes.

Another optical illusion, I guess, fooling trained pilots who spend many hours every working day flying.

There are a number of other occasions on which our military tangled with UFOs and the incidents got hushed up.

In January 1948, Air National Guard pilot Thomas Mantell was killed when his fighter plane crashed while chasing a UFO. Captain Mantell was an experienced pilot with more than two thousand hours in the air and a veteran of the Battle of Normandy.

Mantell took to the air with three other pilots when reports of a large metallic object over the skies of Kentucky came in. The other pilots gave up the pursuit at ten thousand feet, but Mantell continued the chase, and ultimately his plane crashed.

After an investigation, the air force reported that the object that Mantell had been chasing was the planet Venus.

An experienced pilot and war veteran with a couple thousand hours jockeying fighter planes can't tell the difference between Venus and an aircraft?

Was this the first time he had seen Venus, after years of flying?

Four years later, Project Blue Book, an air force investigation of UFO incidents, decided that the Venus chase didn't make sense and changed it. The investigators decreed that Mantell had been chasing . . . what else . . . a *weather balloon.*

What did you expect?

People distant in time and place made a determination that rejected the conclusions of people involved in on-the-spot analysis—and then that decision got rejected and changed by people even further away in time and place.

Another 1948 incident is called the Gorman UFO dogfight. It involved another Air National Guard pilot, George Gorman, but this time it occurred over the skies of Fargo, North Dakota.

Captain Gorman also was a veteran World War II fighter pilot. He was over Fargo in the evening when he (along with others, on the ground and in a civilian plane) spotted what appeared to be a blinking light in the night sky.

Gorman gave chase. The "dogfight" label for the incident refers to the fact that the object he was chasing kept outmaneuvering him, climbing and turning much faster than his P-51 Mustang fighter plane. Gorman later told investigators that a human pilot could not have duplicated the speed and turns of the object and remained conscious.

Air force investigators initially ruled out the possibility that the object was another aircraft or a weather balloon. However, the following year, the air force designated the incident as being caused by a weather balloon.

What about those maneuvers veteran fighter pilot Gorman observed? I don't think weather balloons have jets attached to them.

There were more incidents—so many at what is now Edwards Air Force Base, in the late 1940s, that military personnel were ordered never to talk about "flying saucers."

In what is referred as the Lakenheath–Bentwaters incident, in 1956, military radar in eastern England picked up fast-moving objects that U.S. and Royal Air Force fighter planes scrambled to intercept. Once again, the fighter planes were outmaneuvered and left behind as the luminous objects reached speeds of up to four thousand miles per hour.

However, this particular incident holds an interesting place in the annals of ufology because the government committee that investigated it reported, "In conclusion, although conventional or natural explanations certainly cannot be ruled out, the probability of such seems low in this case and *the probability that at least one genuine UFO was involved appears to be fairly high*" (emphasis added).

No weather balloon cause that time.

58

Another provocative UFO incident that got swept under the carpet involved a commercial passenger jet.

In July 1948, pilot Clarence Chiles and copilot John Whitted were flying an Eastern Airlines passenger plane at about five thousand feet near Montgomery, Alabama. It was a clear night with scattered clouds. Both men were experienced airline pilots and combat veterans.

They reported that a rocket-shaped UFO came at them on a near-collision course. It was a glowing craft about one hundred feet long and twenty-five to thirty feet in diameter. It had a double row of ports or windows radiating bluish-white light and was shooting out a reddish flame exhaust.

The UFO went by the right side of the airliner at a tremendous rate of speed before the pilots lost sight of it in the clouds. They had watched it for about ten to fifteen seconds. Chiles first thought it was a wingless experimental military aircraft and described its shape as similar to the fuselage of a B-29 Superfortress bomber.

The sighting was an electrifying event because it was the first time that two credible sources had gotten close enough to a UFO to get a good look at it.

It was nearly three in the morning, and only one of the passengers reported seeing anything—a man who reported that a bright streak of light had flashed by his window.

Eleven years later, in 1959, the U.S. Air Force investigative agency for UFOs decreed that the UFO was a meteor.

As usual, when the military is dealing with UFOs, hindsight spanning years or decades always seems to be better to them than the eyewitness accounts at the time. But I will give the air force credit this time for originality—at least they didn't say it was a weather balloon.

Just as Roswell became America's most famous and controversial UFO incident, Britain had what is often described as the "British Roswell."

The event involved mostly U.S. Air Force personnel stationed at a Royal Air Force base in England, who saw what they believed to be UFOs. One of the notable facets of the incident is that a senior military officer, the deputy base commander, saw strange lights and supported the UFO conclusion.

Rendlesham Forest is a large recreational woodland in Suffolk, near the east coast of England. Woodbridge, a Royal Air Force base, was nearby. In 1980, the base was utilized by the U.S. Air Force. The deputy base commander was Lieutenant Colonel Charles Halt.

In the wee hours of December 26, 1980, members of a U.S. Air Force night patrol saw bright lights moving in the forest. Three airmen went into the woodland on foot to investigate, believing that a plane had gone down.

The men reported seeing a glowing, metallic-like object that had lights of different colors. It moved through the forest as they approached, while animals on a nearby farm became wildly agitated. A member of the patrol later described the object as a craft of unknown origin.

About an hour later, local police, who had been called to the scene, arrived to investigate. They reported that the only lights they could see by that time were from the Orfordness Lighthouse, miles away on the Suffolk coast.

Air force personnel returned to the forest after dawn to investigate. On the ground, in a small clearing, they found impressions made in a triangular pattern. They also discovered burn marks and broken branches on nearby trees. Two days later, Halt and a team of his men inspected the area and took radiation readings in the triangular area where the depressions had been made. They also took readings of the surrounding trees and bushes.

Several weeks after the incident, Halt wrote a report describing the incident. The report relates how the three airmen went into the forest and observed an object illuminating the whole area with a white light. The report describes the object as being two meters high and two to three meters wide. It had a red pulsating light on top and a bank of blue light underneath.

The object was either hovering above the ground or was on legs.

As the security patrol approached, the object maneuvered through the trees and disappeared. As it did, nearby farm animals went into a frenzy.

About an hour later the UFO was briefly sighted near a base gate.

An examination of the site where the object had been observed revealed deep impressions, where its feet presumably sat down. The impressions in the ground were a foot and a half deep and seven inches wide.

Radiation tests revealed elevated readings both on the ground and in nearby trees.

Later that night, after the radiation tests were done, strange lights were observed in the area for a number of hours. Lieutenant Colonel Halt also observed these lights.

Years later, in 2010, Halt gave a notarized affidavit in which he summarized what had happened and stated he believed that the incident was of an extraterrestrial nature and that it had been covered up by the United States and the United Kingdom. Halt's January 13, 1981, official report and other matters about the incident are available in Wikipedia's "Rendlesham Forest Incident" article.

As with any notable UFO sighting, there are alternative explanations that we need to deal with.

Could the lights have been the lighthouse on the coast? A meteor? Hoax? Hallucination?

The chief suspect, the Orfordness Lighthouse, is about five miles from the military base gate, hardly making it the sort of multicolored, close-up, in-your-face brilliant illumination the air force personnel described. The light can be seen every night, 365 days of the year, so it would not have come as a surprise to the military personnel.

More than one light was observed, and all the lights were described as moving. Neither description fits the beam from the lighthouse.

Was a meteor observed? Meteors move and can generate different colors. But meteors don't hang around, pausing, hovering, or making any of the other gyrations that were observed over hours.

The concept of a UFO hoax by a number of military personnel, including a field-grade officer, during the Cold War is hardly feasible. It is much more likely that it took a great deal of courage to report a UFO incident.

How are the unusual radiation readings explained? And the three-pronged impressions on the ground?

Most importantly, the initial observations were made by military personnel—among them a senior officer who held a high position at the air base. Are we going to simply trash their observations? Don't they deserve to be credited with having accurately described what they saw?

How about the senior officer who believed that his observations and those of his men were being ignored, to the point that he concluded that both the British and the American defense departments were covering up the incident?

Rendlesham Forest is another one of those events in which the observers were not given credit for having seen what they reported, leaving a dark shadow of doubt about the instant conclusion of the British and American powers that be, and about the credibility of the official conclusion that the incident was not extraterrestrial.

59

We are going to fast-forward to 2007, to the most stunning and credible observation of a UFO by an airline pilot. It features the pilot and passengers on a flight over the English Channel, early in the morning but during daylight hours.

The Channel Islands are a chain of islands in the English Channel, between France and England. They are a British dependency. In February 2007, there were reports of unexplained lights in the sky, in a formation pattern, off the coast of the island of Alderney.

About two months later, in April 2007, a British airline pilot, Captain Ray Bowyer, was flying a passenger jet over the English Channel en route to Alderney. Bowyer had eighteen years of flying experience and had been flying this particular route for eight years. The eighty-mile flight started in Southampton on the English coast and terminated on Alderney forty-five minutes later.

The jet was about sixty miles off the coast of England when Bowyer and his passengers spotted two UFOs, which were described as two enormous, seemingly stationary crafts. The UFOs appeared to be identical and emitted brilliant yellow light. Bowyer described the UFOs as being a "flattened disk shape," a "brilliant yellow, with light emanating from within." He indicated that the shape of the UFOs had no relationship to the customary shape of aircraft.

He reported the incident to air traffic control on the island of Jersey. That air traffic control station also got word from the pilot of another plane in the area that he, too, had spotted one of the UFOs.

Further confirmation came that same day from two visitors on the island of Sark. They asked at their hotel about the two bright yellow objects in the sky.

The National Press Club in Washington, DC, is a prestigious organization for journalists and communications professionals. It was founded more than one hundred years ago, and every president since the 1920s has been a member. About six months after the incident Captain Bowyer was invited to speak to the organization. The following is an excerpt from his remarks:

> "My name is Ray Bowyer and I fly a civilian airliner, as captain. I've been invited here, due to my sighting last April of multiple, as yet unidentified, objects over the Channel Islands region of the English Channel. This encounter lasted for fifteen minutes, and the first object being visible from fifty-five miles' distance. On nearing the object, a second identical shape appeared beyond the first. Both objects were of a flattened disk shape with a dark area to [their] right They were brilliant yellow, with light emanating from within, and I estimated them to be up to possibly a mile across. I found myself astounded but curious, but at twelve miles' distance these objects were becoming uncomfortably large, and I was glad to descend and land the aircraft. Many of my passengers saw the objects, as did the pilots of another aircraft, twenty-five miles further south. There is also possible radar information still being investigated. . . . I understand that at this time no definitive solution has been discovered to explain the sighting as yet."

What should we make of the Alderney sighting? It would be easy to write it off as an unusual "atmospheric phenomenon."

But that excuse, so often used by authorities, doesn't play well here. There were no known atmospheric conditions at the time in the area that would have created the phenomenon. Even more significant, the sighting was seen by people from different angles—who reported it as an *object* in the sky.

The eyewitnesses have inherent credibility: two airline pilots, passengers, tourists on the ground, all observing from different angles and with different mind-sets.

Given credible eyewitness testimony and no reasonable alternative explanation, the judge and jury in a court of law would be finding in favor of a UFO sighting.

Which raises another question: What is a UFO? The letters stand for "unidentified flying object," so technically it could mean any object in the sky that can't be identified after a thorough and diligent inquiry. The connotation, of course, is that the flying object is of extraterrestrial origin. In this case, and in most other situations I've investigated, UFOs may be inferred to be of extraterrestrial origin because their size, shape, maneuverability, and/or speed are unlike that of any terrestrial flying object.

Captain Bowyer also noted "differences" in how UFO sightings are reported in Britain as opposed to in the United States, noting that American pilots and witnesses can be pressured not to discuss an incident. He used the example of the Chicago O'Hare Airport UFO incident, so let's take a look at that next.

60

The Chicago O'Hare Airport event Captain Bowyer mentioned is a classic example of the mind-set the government, airlines, and corporations in general have about reports of UFOs. Like three monkeys who turn a blind eye to whatever they don't want to deal with, these entities see no evil, hear no evil, and speak no evil.

O'Hare is one of the busiest airports in the world. The sighting occurred at the airport in November 2006, about four thousand miles away from the Channel Islands and four months before Captain Bowyer and others spotted UFOs over the English Channel.

At a little after four in the afternoon, federal authorities at the airport received a report that twelve airport employees had seen a metallic saucer- or disk-shaped craft hovering over Gate C-17. The strange object was first spotted by ramp workers pushing back a United Airlines flight. The object was observed for a couple of minutes by about a dozen United Airlines employees.

Several people outside the airport also saw the UFO, with one person describing it as having a disk shape and emphasizing that it was an object and not clouds.

The object suddenly shot through the clouds above, leaving a sky-blue hole in the cloud layer.

A strange craft hovering over a terminal at a busy airport in this age of paranoia about terrorists? Sounds like something that cries out for a thorough investigation. The Federal Aviation Administration would get into high gear, the air force would

scramble fighter jets, the president would go on the air to as-
sure the American people and the world that the situation is
under control, congressional committees would start rushing
out subpoenas . . .

Well, perhaps not all that, at least not all at once. But how
about an investigation by the Federal Aviation Administration?
The FAA is the people who control our skies. We would expect them, at the very least, to make sure the skies are safe from
unidentified flying objects.

However, not even the minimum happened. The FAA and
United Airlines in fact denied that the incident had been reported to them, but they changed their tune when the *Chicago
Tribune* hit the feds with a Freedom of Information Act request,
which revealed that a United supervisor had reported the situation to an FAA supervisor at the airport.

The FAA then concluded that the UFO was nothing more
than weather phenomena.

What I find most interesting about the O'Hare UFO incident is not just that the witnesses' employer and the federal
agency charged with the security and safety of our airports and
airways ignored the situation, or even deliberately had employees downplay it, but also that the government determined it was
caused by "weather phenomena."

If the FAA didn't investigate the incident, how did they
know what caused it?

This is what Captain Bowyer told the National Press Club
about the Chicago airport incident and what he has heard about
American pilots being afraid to report UFO sightings:

> "I heard about the multiple-witness sightings at Chicago
> O'Hare Airport, about a year ago now, on November the
> seventh, 2006. I was surprised to hear how it was handled.
> Despite many pilots and airport personnel witnessing the
> object hovering over the terminal, there was no investiga-

tion at all by the FAA. It appears as if pressure may have
been applied to crew members by their company not to discuss this incident. I would have been shocked if I was told
that the CAA [Civil Aviation Authority] in the UK would
obstruct an investigation, or if the CAA told me that what
I had seen was something entirely different. But it seems as
if pilots in America are used to this sort of thing here."

I like Captain Bowyer's description of what he had learned
about the deliberate underreporting of UFO incidents: there
was no investigation by the FAA, "despite many pilots and airport personnel witnessing the object"; "it appears as if pressure
may have been applied to crew members by their company";
and he would be "shocked" if he was told UK authorities had
obstructed an investigation.

If the FAA or the air force isn't interested in investigating a
disk-shaped object capable of soaring away at unearthly speeds
and sitting atop a terminal at one of the country's busiest airports, then who is? Who's in charge of UFOs? The extraterrestrials themselves?

Is that the problem? Extraterrestrials are here. And they are
in charge.

PART IX

THE ABDUCTION PHENOMENON

Have people been abducted by extraterrestrials? Or is that a product of the "abductees" imagination, hallucination, or lies?

We'll take a look at this mysterious phenomenon, starting with what a distinguished Harvard psychiatrist had to say after intensive study of more than one hundred people who claim to have been abducted by extraterrestrials.

Dr. John E. Mack (1929–2004) was a distinguished Harvard professor of psychiatry and a Pulitzer Prize–winning biographer. In an interview with PBS's *Nova*, he finds that people who claim to have been abducted by aliens are pretty credible.

NOVA: Let's talk about your own personal evolution from perhaps skepticism to belief [in alien abduction] . . .
Mack: When I first encountered this phenomenon, or particularly even before I had actually seen the people themselves, I had very little place in my mind to take this seriously. . . .

The idea that we could be reached by some other kind of being, creature, intelligence that could actually enter our world and have physical effects as well as emotional effects, was simply not part of the world view that I had been raised in. So that I came very reluctantly to the conclusion that this was a true mystery. In other words, that I—I did everything I could to rule out other sources, or sexual abuse. Some of these people are abused. But they're able to tell, distinguish clearly the abduction trauma from other forms of abuse. Some forms of psychosis or people making up stories—I could reject that on the basis that there was no gain in this for the vast majority of these people.

I've now worked with over a hundred experiencers intensively. Which involves an initial two-hour or so screening interview before I do anything else. And in case after case after case, I've been impressed with the consistency of the story, the sincerity with which people tell their stories, the power of feelings connected with this, the self-doubt—all the appropriate responses that these people have to their experiences.

—*Nova* online, "Kidnapped by UFOs?" (1996), http:// www.pbs.org/wgbh/nova/aliens/johnmack.html

61

Whodunit?

I love British murder mysteries. But even better than the tales woven by Agatha Christie about a body in the library, or the haunted moors of Arthur Conan Doyle, are the ones tied to the supernatural.

So it shouldn't have come as a surprise to me that one of my favorite mysteries has an *X-Files* twist and is not fiction but an actual British mystery that involves a UFO, alien abduction, cattle that vanish and reappear, a dead body, and a distinguished police investigator.

It began in West Yorkshire, England, in June 1980. The body of fifty-six-year-old Zigmund Adamski was found in a coal yard, a storage area for coal that is sold for heating and cooking. The coal yard was in Todmorden and Adamski was from Tingley, about twenty miles away.

His body was found on top of a large stack of anthracite, hard coal.

He appeared to have died from a heart attack, but the place and condition of the body were swathed in mystery. He had left his home five days earlier to obtain some potatoes, and had then disappeared, but police were not able to determine where he had been during the intervening time—and they were baffled by the totality of the circumstances, which remain unsolved today.

He had no connection to the town or the coal yard.

He was wearing an overcoat and vest, but his shirt, wallet, and wristwatch were missing. His shoes were not tied properly, and an officer who inspected the body believed that the deceased had not tied his own shoes.

He had been alive as recently as eight hours before the body was found, and he could have been on the coal pile only about four or five hours, according to the statement of a witness who had been at the site earlier and then had returned and found the body.

Even though Adamski had been missing for five days, there was nothing about his clothing or physical condition that indicated he had been living in rough conditions or that he had been involved in a violent struggle. He apparently had been shaving regularly during his absence, because he had only one day's growth of beard.

Adamski was found on a pile of coal, but there was no evidence of coal dust, scrapes on his clothes or body, or marks on the coal pile itself that showed how he got to the top of the pile.

The case took a strange turn when mysterious burns were found on the back of his head, neck, and shoulders. The burns had been there for about two days. The medical examiner told the BBC that a strange ointment, which could not be identified by forensics, appeared to have been used on the burns.

How odd—there's something on Earth that can't be identified by forensic scientists?

Was he abducted by aliens, who applied the salve and put him down at the coal yard after he had a heart attack?

No one knows where the burns and ointment came from, but the story isn't finished yet. The mystery of the body found on the pile of coal is going to take an even stranger twist as a connection to an alien abduction plays a part.

Something will happen that causes headlines around the world and gets a British police officer an appearance on *The Tonight Show* with Johnny Carson.

62

It was 4:10 in the afternoon when police officer Alan Godfrey and another officer from the West Yorkshire metropolitan police force arrived at the coal yard in response to the call alerting the police to the body of Mr. Adamski.

Like a character from one of those wonderful British television mysteries, Constable Godfrey had been involved in unusual mysteries before and had twice been commended for his skill in investigating mysterious deaths.

A little over five months after the Adamski investigation ended with unresolved questions, at about five o'clock on November 28, 1980, Godfrey was on duty in a police vehicle on Burnley Road in Todmorden, about a mile from the coal yard where Adamski's body was found. He had been sent out on an unusual assignment: the police had received a number of calls from people who claimed that a herd of cows had been disappearing—and then reappearing.

As he came down the road, Godfrey saw what, at first, he thought was a double-decker bus that had skidded sideways on the road. He flipped on his emergency lights and approached in his vehicle. When he was about seventy-five feet from what he thought was a tall bus, he realized it wasn't a bus—and it wasn't even on the road. It was hovering about five feet off of the ground.

Shaken up, he called for backup on his police radio, but the radio wouldn't transmit. He got the sense that the big object was emanating a force field that was causing the trees on both sides of the road to shake but was not making a sound.

He stayed in the police vehicle and drew a sketch of the strange object, portraying it as a diamond shape with the bottom half rotating and the top part still.

After he finished the drawing, he suddenly found himself driving, twenty or thirty yards past where he had stopped to sketch. A stretch of time had passed, but he had no memory of it. He would later calculate that he could not account for thirty to thirty-five minutes while he had been parked by the diamond-shaped object.

The hovering object was gone.

He examined the ground where the object had been and found the area dry—yet it had rained earlier and the surrounding ground was damp.

Later, with other officers, Godfrey found the missing cows in a field that they could not have gotten into without help, because the only point of access was a locked gate. He was unable to find any marks on the wet ground that showed that the cows had walked to the field.

Godfrey later noticed that he had a mark on his foot and that his boot was split. The next day, three other officers reported seeing strange lights at about the time Constable Godfrey was on the road observing the object.

Although the encounter generated headlines and got Godfrey a guest appearance on Johnny Carson, it caused him embarrassment and he ended up leaving the police agency.

But the story isn't over.

Three years prior to the encounter with the big diamond-shaped object on Burnley Road, Godfrey had been seriously injured when he tried to take three men into custody. He had lost a testicle as a result of being kicked in the groin and was told by his doctor that he would not be able to lead a normal sex life or father children.

Sometime following the UFO encounter, while Mr. and Mrs. Godfrey were in bed, Mrs. Godfrey was awakened by an unusual noise outside the house and was unable to awaken Constable Godfrey. That morning, they had sex for the first time since he had suffered the injury three years previously, and she became pregnant.

I like stories with bizarre twists and happy endings, and this one has both—at least for the Godfreys.

63

The next incident also involves a police officer and is considered one of the most baffling UFO encounters ever reported. What makes this incident so interesting is not only the way the encounter came about and the credibility of the person involved but also that it resulted in an actual piece of evidence that is now in a museum—a 1977 Ford LTD police cruiser.

For this one, we have to leave England and go several thousand miles west, crossing that ocean the British call "the pond," to Marshall County, Minnesota.

It was August 1979, and Deputy Sheriff Val Johnson was on routine patrol, at 1:40 A.M., on a county road. When he came up to an intersection, he spotted a very bright, well-defined light about eight to twelve inches in diameter and three to four feet off the ground.

Johnson's initial impression was that it could be the landing light on an aircraft, perhaps one in trouble. He turned to head in the direction of the light and had gone a little over a mile toward it when the light came directly at his vehicle. It hit and damaged the patrol car, rendering Johnson unconscious.

When the light hit, the patrol car kept going 854 feet south in a straight line, at which point the brakes were applied and its tires left 99 feet of black skid marks on the road. The officer does not know how the car was moved or the brakes were applied.

The patrol car ended up sideways on the road, facing east.

Officer Johnson was unconscious for about thirty-nine minutes. He was taken to a medical facility, where it was found he had "welder" type burns to his eyes.

The damage to the patrol car was all on the left side and the left front and was unusual for an "accident." A headlight was broken, there was a circular dent on the hood and a break in the windshield from several impacts on the driver's side, and two of the car's antennas were bent. The antennas were not bent over from their base. Instead, one shaft was bent forty-five degrees, starting about six inches from the base; another was bent ninety degrees, only near the top; and a third was untouched.

The vehicle's electric clock lost fourteen minutes, as did the officer's wristwatch.

The damage puzzled accident reconstruction experts.

Remember those strange burns and the ointment found on Zigmund Adamski's body, which the coroner said forensic scientists could not identify? In addition to Deputy Johnson's burned eyes, something strange also had happened to the patrol car. The windshield was examined by a Ford Motor Company expert, who concluded that the cracks were created by mechanical forces of an unknown origin and seemed to have been caused by inward and outward forces acting almost simultaneously.

Deputy Johnson appeared on *Good Morning America* but, like Constable Godfrey, he was not pleased by the attention the incident received in the long term.

I started these abduction tales with a quote from a *Nova* interview of the late Dr. John Mack, a Harvard psychiatrist and Pulitzer Prize winner. Mack concluded, after working intensely with more than one hundred people who experienced abductions, that the phenomenon was a true mystery. I don't know whether he ever worked with either Constable Godfrey or Deputy Johnson, but if he had, they certainly would have been star participants, not only because the officers were inherently credible but also because of the evidence that was left behind.

The officers both showed amazing fortitude and bravery in dealing with encounters that would give anyone the shivers.

64

The late 1970s and early 1980s, like the 1940s invasion era, had so many encounters that it seemed as though extraterrestrials were conducting research, putting people under their micro scope to see how the human bugs react when poked with something sharp.

The next incident involves a pilot and a mysterious incident over Australia. But this one ends differently than any of the previous stories.

In October 1978, at about seven o'clock on a clear day, just before night was falling, Australian pilot Frederick Valentich was flying a private plane to pick up friends. En route he radioed air traffic control in Melbourne that a large aircraft that he couldn't identify, with four bright lights, was flying about a thousand feet above him. He told the air traffic controller that the craft was flying over him at high speeds, playing some sort of game with him.

This is from the Australian government transcript of the incident:

Melbourne: Delta Sierra Juliet, can you describe the, er, aircraft?

Pilot: Delta Sierra Juliet, as it's flying past, it's a long shape [*Open microphone for three seconds.*] (cannot) identify more than (it has such speed) [*Open microphone for three seconds.*] (It's) before me right now, Melbourne.

Melbourne: Delta Sierra Juliet, roger, and how large would the, er, object be?

Pilot: Delta Sierra Juliet, Melbourne, it seems like it's stationary. What I'm doing right now is orbiting and the thing is orbiting on top of me also. It's got a green light and sort of metallic, (like) it's all shiny (on) the outside.

He then reported that it was hovering above him—and that it wasn't an aircraft.

That was the last anyone heard from Mr. Valentich. After that, the controller lost contact.

The Department of Transport's aircraft accident investigation summary report stated that, after an "intensive air, sea, and land search," no trace of Mr. Valentich's plane was found. The report was released nearly four years after the incident and did not cite a reason for the disappearance of the plane.

Decades later, skeptics decided that Mr. Valentich, who was an UFO enthusiast, had gotten confused and was flying upside down and being chased by his own lights.

There are two problems with that theory: no trace of the plane was ever found, and eleven witnesses reported seeing a UFO in the area at the time of the radio call.

Reading about the disappearance of this young man, I get an image of that scene in *Close Encounters of the Third Kind*, in which people who had been abducted over the decades come walking out of the extraterrestrial craft.

65

I can't leave this topic without mentioning perhaps the most famous of all cases of alien abduction, that of Betty and Barney Hill.

They were two solid, upstanding citizens, reeking of so much credibility that, along with Deputy Johnson and Constable Godfrey, they could have been poster kids for Dr. Mack's study.

They lived in Portsmouth, New Hampshire, where Betty was a social worker and Barney was an employee with the Postal Service. They were active both socially and in civil rights issues. The encounter took place in 1961, and they had an unusual marriage for the time: they were an interracial couple. Barney was black and Betty was white. This was three years before the Civil Rights Act was passed, in 1964, and a time when some southern states still had laws barring interracial marriages. The Hills were members of the NAACP, and Barney served on the board of the U.S. Civil Rights Commission.

Looking at a picture of this couple, they look very much like the educated, middle-class leaders and pillars of the community that they were. They certainly were not people who would get high on psychedelic mushrooms and imagine that they were seeing flying saucers and those little green people the pope wants to baptize.

Prior to the encounter, Betty and Barney had been on vacation to Niagara Falls and Montreal. It was late at night, about 10:30 P.M., in September 1961. Their return to Portsmouth, which is on the coast, took them through the White Mountains, a densely forested, thinly populated area.

They saw a light in the sky that Betty at first thought was a falling star. But she was puzzled because it moved upward instead of coming down. The Hills parked their car and got out to walk their dog and take a look at the strange light. They took turns looking at the light through a pair of binoculars and observed a craft with multicolored lights. When the object started coming in their direction and Barney realized it wasn't a plane, they got back to the car and continued driving on the isolated road.

The Hills watched the object as they drove. It appeared to be about forty feet long, seemed to rotate, and ran silently. The object moved erratically and then hovered about a hundred feet in front of them. According to Barney, it was shaped like a giant pancake.

When they had gotten out of the car earlier to walk the dog, Barney had taken a gun out of the trunk of their car, in case of bears. He now got out of the car, taking the gun with him, and moved closer to the thing. Using binoculars, Barney observed eight to eleven figures that he "somehow" felt were not quite human, peering out the saucer-shaped craft's windows.

The craft rose to about fifty to eighty feet off the ground and came toward the Hills, until it was about the length of a football field away.

Panicking, the couple got in the car and raced down the road.

They felt the car vibrating and a tingling sensation through their bodies. They experienced an altered state of consciousness, until they became fully alert and discovered that they had traveled about thirty-five miles without realizing it.

Neither of them could recall what happened during the lost time.

Of course, there was an investigation and it came to naught.

This is basically a summary of what happened to the Hills. I provided it to get across a point: The Hills proved in their community that they were people of extraordinary integrity and reliability. They said they saw an extraterrestrial craft a few hundred feet away.

What more could they do to get someone to believe them?

Did they have to shoot it, bag it, and bring it to the nearest sheriff?

66

I saved the "first" abduction for last. It wasn't the very first alien abduction ever reported, but it is the first one that got world-wide attention.

The least that can be said for it is that it is entertaining in a theatrical way—unless you were the abductee!

The incident took place on a farm in Brazil, back in 1957. Antonio Vilas-Boas, a twenty-three-year-old farmer, was plowing a field with a tractor on his family's farm at night to avoid the sweltering daytime temperatures. The farm was in a rural area of São Francisco de Sales, several hundred miles east of Rio.

Antonio and his brother both had noticed white lights in the night sky for several days. While riding on the tractor, Antonio saw what he at first thought was a "red star" in the dark sky. As the object descended toward him it grew in size, until he realized it was a somewhat egg-shaped craft. It had a red light at the front and a rotating dome on top.

As the flying object came down, three legs extended from beneath it as landing gear.

Seeing it coming down near him, Antonio panicked. He tried to flee on the tractor, but he didn't get far, as the tractor's lights faded and its engine died.

He jumped off the tractor and ran. His arm was suddenly grabbed by a small creature wearing a one-piece suit and a helmet. The thing that grabbed him was short, coming up only to his shoulder.

Antonio broke loose from its grip but then was surrounded

by more small figures, who overpowered him and lifted him off the ground. They took Antonio, struggling, into their craft.

The creatures had a human shape, but Antonio was unable to see any features other than their eyes because they all wore a gray uniform that came up to their necks, where the cloth met a gray helmet. The helmet hid all of their features except their blue eyes, which were protected by round glass pieces similar to common eyeglasses. Above the eyes, the helmets extended up a great deal more than a human being's forehead would, making the heads appear to be twice the size of what a human head would be on a body of the same size.

Inside the craft, Antonio's clothes were removed and he was covered from head to toe with a gel he couldn't identify. He was taken through a doorway that had strange red symbols written over it and into an almost circular room. (Antonio was later able to draw the symbols for investigators.)

The humanoids took a sample of Antonio's blood from his chin. Then he was taken to another room and left alone for a short time. Something was pumped into the room, a type of gas, which made Antonio violently ill.

A humanoid creature he had not seen before came into the room, and this one did not have on a uniform. "She" was female and naked. About five feet tall, the same height as the others, she had long, platinum blond hair, blue eyes, and a pointed chin. The hair of her underarms and pubic area was red.

Antonio found her attractive and was sexually aroused. They had sexual intercourse. During their lovemaking she nipped his chin but did not kiss.

After the act was over, the female smiled, rubbed her belly, and pointed upward, a gesture that Antonio took to mean that she was impregnated and that the child would be raised in the beyond.

Antonio was then allowed to dress and was taken on a tour

of the spacecraft. At one point, he tried to take a clock-type device, to have proof of the encounter, but was caught.

He was taken off the ship and it flew off, leaving him alone on the ground. When he got back to the farmhouse, he discovered four hours had passed since he had been abducted.

An aftereffect of the incident was that Antonio suffered a mild dose of radiation poisoning and had unusual bumps and bruises.

Was Antonio abducted and used as a stallion to impregnate a humanoid female? Or did he make up the story?

Only Antonio knows the truth—and that platinum blond being he claims seduced him.

DO YOU NEED ALIEN ABDUCTION INSURANCE?

Alien abduction insurance is a policy issued against alien abduction. The insurance policy is redeemed if the insured person can prove they were abducted by aliens and returned to Earth. GEICO insurance (which does not sell alien insurance policies) and the *Daily Telegraph* report that one English company has sold over thirty thousand policies. Some companies offer policies for alien pregnancy, alien examinations and death caused by aliens.

—"Alien Abduction Insurance," Wikipedia

"A LITTLE TROLL-LOOKING THING"

On a recent broadcast of *Coast to Coast AM*, a night-shift worker at a Missouri lumber mill called to report that something was knocking down fourteen-foot boards in the warehouse. "It ain't no possum," the man drawled. "And it ain't no raccoon." For one thing, it was three feet tall, "a little troll-looking thing, with a big head, and muscular arms . . ." And, the man added, its head wasn't just large; it was *pointed*. And it wasn't wearing any clothes.

Host George Noory listens quietly, acknowledges the strangeness of the man's story, but without snark or judgment. In the histrionic world of talk radio, he's an anomaly: calm, even-keeled, inscrutable. His guests run the gamut from cryptozoologists to psychics to experts on "shadow people." But *Coast* isn't just weird to be weird; it's about pushing your intellectual curiosity to the edge. Case in point: the December 3 show kicked off with an economist, moved to an interview with a UFO abductee, then finished up with a conversation with science writer Harold Bloom, who chatted about physics and his new book, *The God Problem*.

—Stefene Russell, "A Conversation with
George Noory," *St. Louis Magazine*
(January 25, 2013)

ANYTHING GOES

The following is the description of me in a Lowrey High School playbill, from when I played Moonface Martin in the musical *Anything Goes*, featuring the music of Cole Porter.

As you can see, at age sixteen the die was already cast for my career in broadcasting.

George began his career in drama last fall as Lieutenant Guido DiMaggio in *Rally 'Round the Flag, Boys*. He also appeared in Dearborn Civic Theatre's *Carousel*. George is also a member of Lowrey's Men's Glee Club. He is sixteen years old, a junior, and plans on a career in radio and TV broadcasting.

PART X

BEHIND THE VOICE
IN THE NIGHT

A bit about my background is necessary so you will understand how and why I came to the conclusions I have.

67

I'd like to tell you a little about my personal background, so you know why I came to the conclusions I have about life and the world around us.

Because we are all products of a lineage going back thousands of years, to explain myself I need to step back to a time when my forebears found themselves homeless wanderers after they were persecuted in a faraway land for daring to be Christians.

Both my mother's and my father's sides of my family have roots in the Levant, the region bordering the eastern Mediterranean. Neither side of my family is Turkish, but until after the First World War this vast area, and much more, was part of the Ottoman Empire, which once sprawled from Budapest, Hungary, and the gates of Vienna, Austria, almost to the Atlantic Ocean, encompassing the present-day countries of Greece and other Balkan countries, the Middle East, and North Africa.

Following World War I, the clearly defined borders that exist today in that region were not present. The empire fell apart after that First World War and, like millions of others, my grandparents on both sides of my family left behind property, businesses, and family, and became wanderers, stateless and persecuted because they were Christians. Ultimately, America became the home of both sides of my family.

On my mother's side, my grandmother, Ida, was originally married to a man who was murdered during the persecutions of Christians by the Ottoman Turks.

It was a terrible time of war, genocide, and religious and

ethnic massacres, but it was also an era when family bonds, loyalties, honor, and traditions were powerful. Because protecting family was so important, my grandmother's deceased first husband's brother, Seid, married my grandmother, to protect her and the two children she had from that first marriage.

Seid and Ida settled in Fitchburg, Massachusetts, where other members of the family were located. They had children, including my mother, Georgette Margaret Baho, who was born in Fitchburg. Among my uncles and aunts on my mother's side were George, Gabriel, Juliet, Catherine, and Rose.

Like so many others who came to this country after the First World War to avoid the violence and political and economic chaos that gripped so many parts of the Old World, my grandfather Seid was a hardworking immigrant who proved to be a good American, businessman, and provider. He served in the U.S. Army and became a citizen. In addition to providing for his own wife and kids, Seid ultimately provided sanctuary for his mother and for his niece and nephew, whose father had also been killed in a massacre.

In Fitchburg, Seid first worked for a furniture store and then started a business he called Union Furniture Company. The furniture business grew and he added real estate to his business ventures. In later years, my grandfather became quite ill with rheumatoid arthritis, and his sons took over the business and expanded it. During my childhood, my grandfather was restricted to a wheelchair or bed.

Ida also was a hardworking immigrant, a great lady, and a wonderful grandmother.

My grandparents must have been perfect, because they produced Georgette, the best mother on the planet. And that's not just because she's my mother!

My fraternal grandparents had a similar journey to America. Pushed by the winds of war, bedlam, and atrocities in the Levant after the fall of the empire, they made their home for a time in Egypt before coming to the States.

My father was not Egyptian, though he was born in Cairo in 1923. He was born soon after King Tut was awakened from his millennia-long sleep and the curse of the mummy arose. Perhaps that's why a friend, perplexed by my early fascination with the paranormal, accused me of having some of the mystery and magic of ancient Egyptian in my DNA.

As with my mother's family, the wandering in search of a homeland took my father and his family across continents to America. They settled in Detroit, where the American branch of the family was already established.

I never met my paternal grandfather. He passed away before I was born.

The mixture of cultures on all sides gave me a rich heritage of social and religious concepts and beliefs.

The great stock market crash occurred in 1929, a year that was also significant for both my parents.

68

My mother, Georgette, was born in 1929, in Fitchburg, Massachusetts. My father, Gabriel, was six years old in 1929, when he arrived in New York on his way to Detroit from Cairo.

Dad grew up in Detroit and served in the U.S. Army during World War II. He never liked to talk about the war and never elaborated upon his service, but he did once confide that he had seen combat and had had to kill or be killed by enemy combatants.

He was in the Battle of the Bulge, the largest and bloodiest battle fought by the United States in World War II. Prior to his passing, he gave me some of his war memorabilia, including the helmet he wore on the battlefield.

How my father and mother first met is a story of a romance that was meant to be.

After arriving in New York from Cairo, in 1929, my father and his family traveled to Fitchburg to visit my father's uncle before proceeding on to Detroit. The group included my father, his fraternal twin brother, his sister, and his parents.

While in Fitchburg, the family came to my maternal grandparents' house for lunch.

During lunch, the adults noticed that young Gabriel had disappeared. My grandmothers found him in the parlor, standing next to a bassinette. When my grandmother Ida told him he shouldn't be in the parlor because the baby in the bassinette was only a few days old, Gabriel said the baby was holding his finger and wouldn't let go.

The baby, of course, was my mother.

Eighteen years later, my mother was a high school senior when she got on a bus to go to church in Fitchburg.

She recognized an older man (Gabriel's uncle) as an acquaintance of her parents but did not recognize the two young men in their twenties with him. The young men were my father, Gabriel, and his fraternal twin.

My mother didn't know that Gabriel had been the six-year-old whose finger she had hung on to when she was only days old.

Later, back at home, she told her mother that she had seen the uncle with two young men.

That night, the uncle brought Gabriel and his brother over to meet my mother's family. My father and my mother felt an immediate connection as they sat together and talked. Before the night was over, they both realized that they were meant to be together.

My dad had to return to Detroit, but they corresponded frequently.

They were married on August 20, 1949.

I was born June 4, 1950, at Mount Carmel Hospital in Detroit. The delivering doctor was Joseph McGoff. He charged my mother twenty-five dollars for my delivery. I may still have the invoice he gave them.

I was the oldest of three siblings. My sister Gail was born February 28, 1952, and sister Glinda was born May 2, 1958.

With Gabriel, Georgette, George, Gail, and Glinda in the household, friends and relatives called us the "Five G's," and we would get mail addressed to that name.

Naturally, we also had a dog named Giselle.

When I was six, we moved from Detroit to a house in Dearborn Heights, Michigan, which my parents bought in 1956. They paid $14,000 for the small brick house with three bedrooms, kitchen, living room, and basement. It came with a mortgage, but they paid it off within a few years.

My dad, who was called Gabe by people who knew him well, worked for Ford Motor Company in the truck division, as a financial analyst. He stayed there until he retired, when he was sixty years old. In those days, when you had a good job, you didn't leave. He was never really schooled to be an accountant, but that's what he ended up doing, because he was a numbers guy.

He was a good provider, for whom family came first. Just as he and my mother were meant to be, he also loved his kids. He was the ultimate family man, available to take us wherever we needed to go. He was not someone who played golf on the weekends or met up with pals at the local watering hole. He preferred being home with the family, reading the newspaper, enjoying my mother's cooking, and working in the yard.

He kept the grass and the rest of the yard perfect and was always after me to get into yard work with as much enthusiasm as he did. I did my share but I didn't have a green thumb. And, knowing how particular he was about his plants, one notable disaster put me into a panic.

My dad had planted a peach tree in the backyard. The tree was four or five feet tall and blooming beautifully. Unfortunately, it got in the way when a friend and I were playing ball, and it cracked in the middle.

We decided to patch it up and put tape around it, using tape the same color as the bark. The deception lasted a few days, and then the leaves started looking wilted and began falling off. Dad looked at it from the kitchen window and muttered that it looked like it was dying. Naturally, the repair job didn't pass muster when he got up close.

Fortunately, my father was not a strict disciplinarian. My sister Gail says our parents were lucky we were good kids and never gave them much of a hard time growing up, and I guess it worked both ways.

Dearborn Heights is a middle-class suburban community right outside of Dearborn. It was a nice place to grow up, with a good school system. I walked just a couple of blocks to Pardee Elementary School, played baseball and other sports after school, and hung out with a group of friends who remind me of the boys in *Stand by Me.*

In some ways, while growing up I was closer to my mom than to my dad, because she took more interest in the things that interested me. It was my mom who taught me how to play baseball, by pitching balls to me in the backyard, and how to ride a bike. When, at an early age, I became enthralled with both science and the paranormal, she bought me a telescope and a book about extraterrestrial life.

Dad was a hard worker, a great provider, and a terrific family man who took an interest in my career plans as I got older, but he wasn't the kind of father who taught a kid how to play sports on the weekend. Though he did try. One time, when I was in the Boy Scouts, he came along on a camping overnighter. In the morning he said, "Georgie, I'm driving back home. I can't handle this." Off he went.

My mother claims she was sometimes overprotective of me, and I love to tell the story of a water fight that took place when I was seven or eight and three kids attacked me with squirt guns. It was a hot summer day and I should have relished it, but instead I ran home and cried to my mother. "Mom! Mom! They're shooting at me with squirt guns!"

My mother was both imaginative and inventive. Pretending to be a peacemaker, she told me to invite the kids over for Kool-Aid. I said no, I don't want them over, but she said do it, so I ran across the street, getting pelted again, and invited the kids over for Kool-Aid. When the kids got over to the house, my mom came out from hiding with a bucket of water and drenched them. She protected her little boy Georgie back then, and she still does today.

69

I was raised Roman Catholic, singing in the choir and going to catechism classes.

I went to the public school system in Dearborn and Dearborn Heights: Pardee Elementary School, O. W. Best Middle School, and Lowrey High School.

Through much of high school I worked, selling shoes at Bakers Shoes, bagging groceries, and whatever else I could find.

At Lowrey High I played on the football and baseball teams, wrote for the school newspaper, was in the glee club, and was voted most talented by my peers—probably because I participated in just about everything.

I was in nearly every play that the school put on. I really enjoyed acting in the plays and musicals, playing the role of the Kralahome, the prime minister, in *The King and I*; of Guido DiMaggio in *A Pennant for the Kremlin*; and of Fagin in *Oliver*. In *Anything Goes*, I played a singing criminal called Moonface Martin.

I was eleven when I had my first encounter with the paranormal.

I had a good track record of never getting sick and never missing school, but one day I woke up with a fever and had to stay home in bed. As I was lying there, I suddenly realized that I wasn't on the bed but was way above it, up at the ceiling— and I was looking down at my own body.

I hovered there in the air, suspended above the bed, looking down curiously at my still body on the bed.

I first thought I was dreaming, but that wasn't it. I was out of my body, or at least my conscious mind and essence were out, hovering in midair. It was an eerie sensation, because I was wide awake yet I could see my sleeping body.

At some point my consciousness took over and slammed me back into my body.

The experience left me full of questions. How could my sense of consciousness leave my body and permit me to observe my own physical form? Was it possible my conscious mind could just fly away and leave my body forever?

Today there is much more awareness about out-of-body experiences (OBEs) than there was back in the sixties, because of instant access to information about anything and everything through the Internet. Back then, if you told people your mind had briefly slipped free of your body and floated around, people would assume you had experienced an LSD trip.

I was puzzled and intrigued enough to make a trip to the library to research what I had experienced. I found a book by Hereward Carrington and Sylvan Muldoon called *Projection of the Astral Body*, which had been published in 1929. It turned out that this is the seminal treatise on the subject.

In the book, Sylvan Muldoon writes about his own out-of-body experience, which occurred when he was twelve years old, about my own age. He had awakened in the middle of the night unable to move. Lying in bed, paralyzed, he knew who he was but was not aware of where he was. He felt himself moving, but it was his conscious mind that moved, while his physical body remained on the bed.

He went from being unable to move to experiencing a sensation of floating and looking down at his own body on the bed.

Frightened, he tried to get to the next room to wake up other people and found that he passed right through his closed door and then through other doors and walls. When he tried to wake up other members of the family by shaking them, his hand passed right through them.

After being free of his body for about fifteen minutes, he gradually reconnected with it.

I read the book and realized that Muldoon's experience of hovering and looking down at his own body was what had happened to me.

Reading the explanation in the book, by someone who had actually had an out-of-body experience, was both a relief and a revelation to me. I wasn't crazy. I wasn't dreaming or hallucinating.

This OBE caused me to make a couple more discoveries about life at an early age.

70

A 1968 university study of an out-of-body experience revealed that the subject had had a previous OBE, and that this had been a shocking situation for the subject, rather than simply being a physical experience.

The subject of the study was a woman in her twenties who had experienced out-of-body incidents in the past. During the four-night study, she reported OBEs. The researchers found a correlation between her reported out-of-body experiences and the physiological data gathered during the incidents, such as a flattened EEG reading and no rapid eye movement.

The abstract of the scientific article states, "Two incidents occurring in the laboratory provide suggestive evidence that the out-of-the-body experiences had parapsychological concomitants" (Charles T. Tart, "A Psychophysiological Study of Out-of-the-Body Experiences in a Selected Subject," *Journal of the American Society for Psychical Research* 62, no. 1: 3–27). It's fascinating that the university doctors gathered enough evidence of OBEs to warrant further research into the "parapsychological" aspects of the phenomenon.

However, the young woman's reported previous experience had more of a nightmarish than a paranormal slant. I mention it because it shows a dark side to out-of-body experiences, which is not ordinarily reported.

As is true of some people who experience out-of-body incidents, this woman sometimes left the house during her OBEs and traveled a considerable distance, rather than just floating above her body.

Edgar Cayce was noted for going into a trance and sometimes traveling a great distance out of his body to examine a patient.

When she was about fourteen years old, the woman had what amounted to a vivid nightmare, or a nightmarish OBE, as she found herself walking down a dark, deserted street in the town where she lived. As she walked, she realized that she was in someone else's body and was wearing that person's checkered shirt.

She became terrified as she realized someone was following her.

I'm not going into the details of what she reported happened, because they are gruesome, but basically the stalker grabbed her and murdered her.

A couple of days later, the news media reported that a young woman had been brutalized in the same manner that the subject with the OBE had envisioned.

The victim had been wearing a checkered shirt.

A phenomenon that has a close relationship to an OBE is a near-death experience, a type of out-of-body experience that occurs when the subject is clinically dead and recalls the experience after being resuscitated.

"Clinically dead" means that at some point there was no heartbeat or breathing, even if you are revived thereafter. There also have been near-death experiences reported when the patient was actually brain dead and then was later revived.

Near-death experiences are not a recent phenomenon. In Plato's *Republic*, written more than two thousand years ago, Er, a soldier who was believed to be dead, was put on a funeral pyre to be cremated but was then revived and described his journey into the afterlife.

Er is not alone in seeing images during death and revival—

about a third of the people who "die" and are revived experience a near-death experience. That amounts to millions of people in America alone.

Many of the visions have been spiritually enlightening. There are so many similarities among the visions that people have while technically "dead" that it is difficult to simply write it off as imagination gone wild.

71

The fact that my out-of-body experience was an unusual event that not everyone experiences didn't matter. Like most things in life, no one's path is a duplicate of everyone else's. People are different; things can and do happen to the few that never occur for the many.

Nor did categorizing it as a paranormal incident make it any less real or credible to me. "Paranormal" only means that someone has not verified it with a scientific test or instrumentality.

Even when tests are done, most scientists will naturally try to reconcile the results with generally accepted theories rather than with concepts that do not have almost universal acceptance.

I knew what I had experienced, knew I had not been asleep at the time. I also realized that I was not the only one who had experienced an out-of-body incident. It had happened to Muldoon, who set out to study the phenomenon and discovered that many other people had experienced it.

Today, after decades of experience and working with others on a wide range of subjects, I know for certain that not everything can be verified by science. Not by a long shot. Scientists are still trying to figure out even the fundamentals about human existence and the planet we live on—how the world and people on it came to be in the first place.

And I had learned that there are resources I could use to investigate a happening. Of course, in those days, my feet did the walking to a library, rather than my fingers walking on a computer keyboard. Despite all my criticism of the Internet for the potential damage that can result from it, no one can question what an incredible source it is for knowledge.

The most significant thing I learned was to question things and to investigate them when my experiences didn't coincide exactly with what everyone else seemed to be saying. That was especially true when it came to science.

I believe in science. I trust science, for the most part. But anyone with a sense of history knows not only that science doesn't have *all* the answers but also that, periodically, entire fields of science get turned upside down by some future Nobel Prize winner who upsets the apple cart by suddenly revealing whole new truths.

From the moment my conscious mind hovered overhead and stared down at my corporeal self, I was open to the concept that some truths are stranger than fiction. I loved the notion of ghosts, restless spirits who never fully departed; or that big, strange-looking creature that people sometimes spotted in the distance or found huge footprints of, called Sasquatch, Bigfoot, or Yeti.

There were creatures of all kinds that science hadn't studied, and people who possessed amazing powers that science could not explain—magic, extrasensory perception, telepathy, remote viewing, dream states, clairvoyance, telekinesis, and mind over matter in endless ways.

The paranormal was not just stranger than fiction but also utterly fascinating. What an exciting realm! What thought-provoking and electrifying ideas were available when I opened my mind to them!

My out-of-body experience and a compelling fascination with the paranormal was just the beginning. A couple of years later, when my mother asked me what I wanted for Christmas, I told her I wanted Walter Sullivan's *We Are Not Alone*. I didn't know it at the time, but reading that book, even as young as I was, would take me from just having a worldview to one that encompassed the whole universe.

My mother got me the book, which at that time was controversial and provocative because of its theory that there is other life in the universe besides us earthlings—an idea which, today, is pretty generally accepted. Another whole new world had opened for me. I was already enthralled with the things and beings found outside the narrow confines of science—the paranormal. Now I was just as fascinated by the concept that scientific evidence pointed to the existence of life on other planets.

I begged my mother for a telescope, and she took me out and bought me a good one. I'm sure that, at the time, she was hoping the telescope would start me on a career path in science and eventually winning a Nobel Prize.

She was right that the doors opening up for me were going to send me on a career path, but it was going to be one centered around the things that science seemed to ignore or denigrate as lacking importance.

My interest also was in peeking into places that science had never been.

72

While still an adolescent, in the sixties, I joined the National Investigations Committee on Aerial Phenomena (NICAP), a nonprofit organization dedicated to doing research on uniden tified flying objects. I was drawn to the organization because it had a reputation for approaching UFO sightings as deserving scientific investigation. It also had an impressive number of scientific and military experts among its membership.

From its founding in the fifties, the organization was noted for having a profound suspicion that the government was concealing information not just about the existence but also about the presence of extraterrestrials. In retrospect, looking at all the evidence of visits from the beyond that was available back in the forties, it's not hard to understand why, from very early on, there was well-founded suspicion that evidence of extraterrestrial visitation—and even what I call "invasion"—was being covered up.

One of the key things I first realized about UFOs was that the government seemed to dither, vacillating between degrees of flustered excitement, as a military officer reported an instance of visitation in Roswell, or other sightings, followed by fearful denials of the information released. Even back then it was obvious to NICAP members that the investigation into UFO sightings was not being conducted in a reasonable manner.

Among those tough subjects that science avoids and ignores, UFOs rank high on the list.

I can't say that my mother encouraged my bent toward the supernatural, but she certainly fed it. She is a spiritual person, but she has a very open mind when it comes to the paranormal and extraterrestrial life. This was unusual, because back in the sixties awareness that there were places science had never gone was rarer than it is today.

Another publication that generated a lot of interest for me was a *Look* magazine excerpt of the book called *The Interrupted Journey*, about the abduction of the New Hampshire couple Betty and Barney Hill. It is an amazing story related by people with a great deal of credibility. I spoke about their encounter earlier, and I'm sure you can imagine the effect this story had on me. Betty and Barney Hill were people who were highly unlikely to lie about or even exaggerate what happened.

I couldn't get enough of the supernatural. Besides reading about UFO incidents and joining NICAP, I read everything I could get my hands on, including Edgar Cayce, the father of holistic medicine, who, as I've mentioned, was called the Sleeping Prophet because of his ability to predict events and diagnose medical problems.

My father was a very practical numbers guy, with a talent for accounting, and was not at all into the paranormal. However, I had that "aunt," the late neuropsychiatrist Dr. Shafica Karagulla, who was a very distinguished authority in the field of out-of-body incidences and whom I was able to speak to and get advice from.

Even though her journey through life covered a lot of territory, when I knew her she was a Los Angeles–based neuropsychiatrist who had become fascinated with brain states and consciousness after her case studies uncovered conclusions that extended the foundations of contemporary knowledge about human awareness.

I had access to her works when I was a teenager, and I was fascinated by her theories of higher states of awareness, clairvoyance, telepathy, out-of-body experiences, and other subjects that would be "taboo" to most psychiatrists. In addition, she was a very prestigious neuropsychiatrist, both as a practitioner and scientist.

At the same time that I was an adolescent enthralled with the supernatural, I was also participating in many public school functions, playing sports, writing for the school paper, performing in plays, going to catechism classes, and singing in the glee club and the church choir.

Someone once asked me if I ever had a discussion with a priest about whether there is life on other planets. My reply was that I never had that discussion because the subject matter never came up in church. But I would tell my science teachers that there was life on other planets, and this was long before the first exoplanets were discovered, in 1992. My "textbook" for extraterrestrial life back in the sixties, of course, was *We Are Not Alone*.

Even though I had become obsessed with unexplainable phenomena at an early age, it didn't keep me from also developing an interest in science. I loved science courses at school and did my own "science" at home, in the basement, where I built Estes model rockets that my friends and I launched, sometimes putting little frogs in capsules that came down with a parachute.

I had listened to Edward R. Murrow and Walter Cronkite on radio and television and had a habit of making "news" announcements—like the liftoff of toy rockets—to the neighborhood kids, broadcasting the launches to friends, who would gather around in the old school park.

My buddy Gary Frank would put the little electrodes in the solid propellant engine and hit the button when I said "Zero," and off the rocket would go.

I built rockets and went into broadcasting, while Gary ended up helping to build the engines for the space shuttle.

I had friends, played a lot of sports, learned the trumpet and guitar, but I enjoyed doing my little science stuff mostly on my own. Besides my rocket stuff, I had a chemical set, a telescope, and hamsters in the basement. I pretty much kept my interest in NICAP and extraterrestrials to myself. Most of the kids I knew were only interested in aliens that came out of Hollywood movies and had ray guns or long tentacles.

I joined a telescope club. My mother tells me she would get up late at night, look out the kitchen window, and see me with my telescope in the backyard.

A part of me loved the supernatural and another part loved science. This was pre–*Star Wars* and the glamorization of science. Cowboys with six-shooters and horses were still the norm for young people, rather than space cadets with ray guns.

With my telescope, chemistry set, and dissecting kits, I was a little mad scientist down in the basement. And the "science" at least once went south—because of a hamster.

I loved hamsters and I decided I was going to breed them, because I wanted to see what happened. So I went ahead and bought a male and a female. I learned that you can't put the male into the female's cage or she will devour him. In order to get her pregnant, you have to put her in his cage and then take her out after they do their little thing.

I predicted, to the exact day, when the little hamsters would be born, and I was right. You have to not disturb the babies because, if you do, the mother eats them to protect them. And I did that all right, left them alone, and had them in their cage.

In those days we had one bathroom upstairs and one down in the basement. My father used the downstairs bathroom every morning to shave. One morning, I remember him screaming at the top of his lungs—*screaming for me*. I woke up, flew out of bed, and ran down to the basement.

Oh, no! One of the little hamsters, about an inch long, had slipped through the cage fencing. Naturally, my dad had stepped on it. Worse, the squishy-squiggly little thing had stuck on the bottom of his foot. And he was just horrified—*horrified*.

I said I didn't know how it had happened, but a quick glance at the hamster cage confirmed that the fencing was too wide to keep in the little guys.

73

When I was eighteen, I entered the University of Detroit, a Catholic university associated with the Jesuits. The school was close enough to home that I didn't run the expense of living on campus. My dad had given me an old Mercury for transportation.

The university had a premier dental school and I entered with a pre-dental course of study.

Why pre-dental for a guy who would end up spending almost his entire career in broadcasting? For the same reason I'm sure many young people end up in majors that don't fit them: I did it to please my father. There are a surprising number of dentists in our family circle and, in my father's eyes, being a dentist was a profession that would provide me with a good foundation in life.

In those days, you could go to dental school after fulfilling the first two years of undergraduate pre-dental. I stayed the course for about a year and a half, preparing to spend the rest of my life as a dentist, but I had also been taking some broadcasting classes because the pre-dental curriculum bored me.

It was hard to study a subject I had no interest in, hard to keep up the pretense that I liked the notion of spending the rest of my life as a dentist when I had no interest in the field. I didn't want to disappoint my dad but I was bored out of my mind, except in broadcasting-related classes.

The issue came to a head when a student I met in a broadcasting class asked if I wanted to fill in for him as a copy boy/production assistant at a television station. I didn't realize it when the question was asked, but the answer to the question would put me on an entirely different path than the one I had been on.

74

I was nineteen in 1969, when David Wittman told me he wanted to go home to Cleveland over the Christmas break and asked if I was interested in doing his production assistant job at the television station for two weeks. His boss had told him he had to find a backup who could do the job or else David wouldn't be able to go home for the holidays.

David was working at WXYZ-TV channel 7 in Detroit, which back then was an ABC station. He approached me at school and said, "Look, George, I know that you like broadcasting, that you're really into it. Do you want to replace me for two weeks at the station?"

Interested? I felt like a wannabe astronaut being asked if he'd like to fill in for a trip to the moon.

I thought, *Wow, this is something I really want to do,* and here was a chance to take a swing at it. Of course I jumped at the opportunity.

"Heck yeah!" I told David.

There was a catch, of course: I had to be interviewed by the station's news manager. I went through the interview and the news manager told me I had the job for a couple of weeks while David was gone.

I went to work at the station with the same work ethic I already had and would keep right up to today: giving 120 percent every single day.

What's a copy boy—or, using a more modern, politically correct label, a production assistant—do? Get 'em coffee; clean the teletype machine (they had ink ribbons in those days); fetch the rundowns of shows and photocopy them; run back and forth at the station, doing this and that as demanded by that person and the other; drive all over Detroit picking up film canisters from cameramen so the film could be developed and broadcast. They didn't shoot video out the field in those days but on sixteen-millimeter film.

I operated at a frantic pace the whole time. Some people looked at me like I was a wild man. I made the magnificent sum of two dollars an hour, but I would have paid them for the experience!

David came back to his job, but people went to the boss and said, *Keep George, too.* The news director called me in and asked whether I wanted to stay and work part time and I said I sure did. So the station kept both of us on.

I guess it's pretty much like starting in the mailroom, but to me it was heaven. I loved the energy and excitement of the broadcasting world. And the hook I had swallowed was dug deep in my soul.

At the university, I talked to a counselor and switched my major. I didn't tell my father because I didn't want to disappoint him. But I also couldn't keep up a charade for long because it was on my conscience.

So one day I came home and got up the courage and told my father that I had no interest in being a dentist.

"I've changed majors."

Up to this time, about the only "serious" father–son crises we'd suffered were the broken peach tree and the squashed hamster.

He stared at me for a long moment and then asked, "What did you change it to? Engineering?"

Uh, no, it wasn't engineering. "Communications," I told him.

"Communications? What does that mean? What kind of career is that?"

"Broadcasting, Dad. I want to go into broadcasting."

He didn't talk to me for two months.

Communications. Broadcasting. Those were words without meaning to my dad. His generation, and that of his parents, had had their lives pulled out from under them. They wanted their children to have something solid to hang on to when the world shifted under their feet.

My dad had a good work ethic. Keeping a roof over our heads and food on the table by getting and staying at a good, solid job, even if it wasn't the thing he would most love to do, was important to him.

I could see his point even back then. Not only was there nothing wrong with dentistry but also it was a much safer bet.

It just wasn't me.

There's an old song from the World War I era that I probably heard in a movie. It seemed appropriate to the situation. It was called "How Ya Gonna Keep 'Em Down on the Farm (After They've Seen Paree)?".

75

Through most of high school, I was pretty busy with everything but girls. That changed when I was a senior and fell for a hot redheaded junior.

My first date became my high school sweetheart and turned out to be the woman I married, although it took a couple of years for us to get to the wedding bells stage.

Her name is Lucinda. We called her Cindi. I was eighteen and she was seventeen when we went on that first date. It was the sex, drugs, and rock-and-roll sixties and early seventies. We weren't into that scene, but I added being in love to my activities.

I was twenty and she was nineteen in 1970, and we were very much in love when we decided to get married. The wedding took place at Saint Albert the Great Catholic church in Dearborn Heights. It was our parish church, where I had sung in the choir and had catechism classes. The wedding reception was small and took place at my parents' home.

Cindi and I got a little apartment in Taylor, Michigan, which is near Dearborn Heights. I think the rent was two hundred dollars a month. The marriage obviously came with financial burdens for us, as it does for most people.

After the marriage, my parents worried I would leave school, and they begged me to finish. They didn't realize how committed I was to getting my degree. But something had to give, financially, and I knew I had to work full time if we were going to make it, even though Cindi was a hard worker who also held down a job. Like me, she was always busy. She was a hospital candy striper in high school, worked at an allergy clinic, and held other jobs.

I was a part-time copy boy/production assistant making two dollars an hour. That wasn't going to keep the proverbial roof overhead and the blazing hearth going for very long.

76

When I got married, I was still a copy boy/production assistant at the WXYZ-TV station. I worked the assignment desk, a position I had been doing since I was nineteen.

The assignment desk moved the TV reporters and crews around, sending them to news conferences, events, and other newsworthy happenings. Working the desk included listening to the police monitors for crimes, accidents, and emergencies we should cover. It was an important job because, in most ways, the person at the assignment desk was in charge of the newscast.

The news director knew I needed to make more money and that I wanted to be a reporter, even though I was exceptionally young in comparison to other reporters. The TV reporters at the station back then were pretty much all old-time newspaper and other printed media veterans.

In those days nobody thought about demographics. No one said, *Hey, let's hire a nineteen-, twenty-year-old kid to appeal to a younger audience.*

One day the news director comes in and says, "George, you're never going to get hired as a radio reporter unless you have a good audition tape. So let's do it."

"When?" I asked.

"Right now."

So we just walked across the hall to the radio station, which was in the same building as the TV station, and to a recording area.

He handed me a news story and said, "Read this."

He recorded me reading it aloud.

"That's pretty good, but why don't you read it again."

And I did. And he said that version was good, too. And, for some stupid reason, I said, "Well, do I get the job?"

"George, I don't have a job for you. I want you to go out and get one. I'll give you copies of your demo tape and you call up stations and make appointments with the news directors."

So I did. And the first place I called was WCAR radio, Detroit.

The news director's name was John Webster, and he told me to bring over my tape.

I brought him the tape and, after listening to it, he said, "I need you as my reporter, full-time, at one hundred forty-six dollars a week."

Life was good. I was making $146 a week as a radio news reporter, at the age of twenty-one, in 1971. I thought I'd hit the mother lode.

But there was a problem with working all day: I was going to school full-time during the day. But my boss told me, "You're going to have to switch your classes to evening ones if you want to continue going to college."

To stay in school, I changed my class schedule to nights and worked at the radio station during the day. I paced myself so that I was able to finish college and get my degree in a customary four-year framework.

Our daughter Wendy came along, and I was comfortable being a father, student, and worker.

Even though we had the baby to care for, college to complete, and a roof to keep over our head, we didn't have a lot of fear, perhaps because we were both used to working. Wendy was an adorable little girl, cuter than a button, and we didn't miss a beat at school, work, our marriage, or caring for her.

My sister Gail told me that I appeared to have matured fast after the marriage, that when my dad and I attended her Father and Brothers Weekend sorority event, I appeared to be in a different place than other young men my age who attended, because I was a husband and father myself. She thought I missed out on a lot of youthful craziness, and maybe that was true, but I was just happy that Cindi and I managed to keep our heads above water and were moving forward.

I don't feel I missed anything other than some sleep, during my college days, because I immediately got busy with family and work.

77

At this point, what some people might call a weird coincidence occurred: my first real radio interview, ever, was with a ufologist, in 1971.

Stanton Friedman is a nuclear physicist who has worked for many of the world's technology giants, including General Electric, Aerojet General Nucleonics, McDonnell Douglas, and Westinghouse. He is also a noted ufologist, a researcher and investigator into unidentified flying objects phenomena. He has provided congressional testimony about evidence suggesting that Earth is currently and has been in the past visited by extraterrestrials. He has twice appeared before the United Nations and has spoken at hundreds of colleges and professional groups.

So, was it an incredible coincidence that the new young reporter who was enthralled by the paranormal launched his radio reporting career by interviewing one of the biggest guns in the field? Was it an act of God, a miracle, because I had obediently gone to catechism when I was a kid?

Actually, it was neither coincidental nor miraculous. It was the result of devious planning on my part. I had spotted a little clip in the *Detroit News* that a UFO expert was going to be speaking at Oakland University, north of Detroit, and it rang bells in my head. I wanted to cover the story.

My news director didn't want me doing a UFO thing, so I ended up interviewing Stanton Friedman on my own.

It was a great start for me, because one of the reasons I wanted to go into broadcasting was to investigate and cover paranormal stories, and I figured that people would talk to a reporter about their experiences before they would talk to somebody on the street.

Although I was off to a good beginning, with that first interview, to fulfilling my dream of enmeshing myself in the paranormal, it would be decades before I was dealing with my fascination on a daily basis, because even though I was excited about the weird and unexplained, broadcasting executives and advertisers who controlled what went on the air were not ready for it.

Life is a circle, of course, and Stanton Freidman became a frequent guest on my radio show, more than thirty years after that 1971 radio interview.

78

Continuing to work and attend college full time, I graduated from the University of Detroit's College of Liberal Arts and Education in 1972 with a degree in communications—not dentistry or engineering.

I brought Wendy to graduation and she sat on my lap, wearing my graduation hat.

Another significant event occurred in 1972: my draft lottery number came up as twenty. I was fully prepared to serve, but I failed the physical, due to a rapidly beating heart and a heart murmur.

The heart condition had been discovered when I was sixteen and working part-time as a bagger in a grocery store. I bent down to pick up a bag and, when I straightened back up, my heart started beating rapidly. It was scary, but I was able to slow my heartbeat down by staying calm and taking deep breaths until the rhythm came back. We were never able to figure out exactly what caused it—probably a little electrical malfunction—but it eventually went away.

Even though I was rejected for the draft, I received a Navy Reserve commission in 1981 and stayed nine years.

By 1973, I was antsy to move on, even though I enjoyed working as a radio news reporter. I wanted to return to television in a position of responsibility, and I set my eye on being a television news producer.

Basically, the job consists of putting the newscast on the air at the particular time period. Let's say there's a six o'clock evening newscast. The news producer is responsible for working with the talent who will deliver the news, the engineers, the assignment people, and just about anyone else who is needed to get the news on the air at six o'clock—and to make sure it stays on the air right up to the end of the program's sign-off. I would have to determine what to lead the show with, figure out how to get people in and out and off on time, deal with the reporters inside and in the field, and decide how long the piece should run.

I had heard from a reporter who worked at WWJ-TV channel 4 in Detroit (which is now WDIV) that the station was looking for a producer. Getting the job would be a major career move. At that time, it would have been huge for me, my entrée back into television not as a copy boy but as a news producer.

I called the WWJ news director and wangled an interview. The interview went well and I got hired immediately.

I don't remember exactly what the pay was, probably twenty thousand dollars a year or something like that, but this was 1973 and I was fresh out of college, stepping into a job where I had an opportunity to show my abilities to manage news, so I felt like I had won the lottery.

Two very important things in my life happened the following year, 1974. My daughter Kristina was born, and I took a job with another Detroit television station, WJBK channel 2, as the eleven o'clock news producer. It was a higher-level position than the news producing I had been doing. That meant more pay, more challenge.

We left the rented apartment and bought a little house. It came with a mortgage, of course. It was southwest of central Detroit, in Taylor, Michigan, on Statler Street, a new subdivision.

I had changed jobs three times between 1971 and 1974, moving up in broadcasting each time, and I started doing the same with houses. After the Taylor house, in 1977, we bought a house in Farmington Hills, and then, also in 1977, we turned around and bought a twenty-acre farm in Fowlerville.

Why the twenty-acre farm? Quite a change. It was something I had always wanted to do, and we went ahead and bought it, even though it was more than fifty miles from Detroit and Dearborn Heights.

I didn't realize it at the time, but this was the beginning of a disaster for me with Cindi. She was stuck a long way out in the middle of nowhere when I went to work every night as a television producer. At that time, we only had one car, so she was literally trapped. It created some tension for us.

Adding to the strain, my little Honda Civic kept breaking down in the winter. I think maybe I was the first person to notify Honda that the Civic accumulated some sort of water vapor by the fuel pump or something. It would cough and sputter every time it either rained or snowed. Maybe they resolved that issue because of me, but I'm not sure.

We had to sell the farm. Cindi just wasn't happy there. Unfortunately, we sold it without realizing that we had acres of valuable black walnut trees on it. I guess farming wasn't for us.

In 1975, as news producer, I arranged an interview with former Teamsters president Jimmy Hoffa. It took place a month before his disappearance became one of the unsolved mysteries of the twentieth century. I had one of my news guys, Wally Scott, do the interview.

Despite Hoffa's reputation as a tough guy with links to organized crime, I was impressed by him. I thought he was a no-nonsense guy, although I really didn't understand the full significance of his background until I saw the Jack Nicholson movie in which he played Hoffa.

Hoffa said he wanted to come back to the union presidency, which was against his parole terms, but he said that's what he wanted to do anyway.

That's what *he* wanted, but the Mob obviously didn't want him back in, because he wasn't going to play ball with them anymore.

Hoffa is a person of history, and his disappearance has even grown a shadow of supernatural mystique around it as government authorities dig here and there to find him, following one hot tip and then another every few years.

In 1978, our reporting of the Detroit/Midwest blizzard was awarded an Emmy. I was very proud of the way we set it up, covered it, and presented it on the air. The Emmy committee agreed and picked it as the best of the breaking news stories of that year.

I stayed at the television station from 1974 to 1978, leaving with the title of Executive News Producer and going to Minneapolis to become news director for television station KMSP-TV channel 9. That meant moving to another state with our young family.

It was a necessary move for my career. Being an executive producer in Detroit made me second banana in the news operation, under the news director. In Minneapolis, as news director, I would be in charge of the whole operation, doing everything from hiring to editing, everything it takes to get the news broadcast.

The move resulted in more pay, more status, more duties, all of which played into the decision by Cindi and me to take ourselves and our young children, Wendy and Kristina, away from family and friends in Detroit.

Both Cindi and I liked Minneapolis, so the move played well on that level, too.

We bought a house in Eden Prairie, which was an up-and-coming suburb at the time.

The move made me the youngest major market news director in the country at the time, and it was a great stepping stone.

I had been courted by NBC to work at some of their own

television stations, in either Los Angeles or New York, but I was a kid from the Midwest and I just wasn't used to that kind of huge city lifestyle, and neither was Cindi. So I elected to go to Minneapolis.

Things started unraveling almost immediately in Minneapolis.

79

That I had stepped into a potential mess in Minneapolis came home a couple of weeks after I got there, when the KMSP-TV channel 9 general manager called me in to his office. The station was an ABC affiliate. He told me I had been brought in to try and save the station's news department, because ABC, as a network, was not happy with the quality of the department.

I said yes, I knew that, and that's what we were trying to do.

He said he knew I'd only been there two weeks, but ABC had decided to yank its affiliation with the station. It was moving its affiliation to the NBC station in Minneapolis. The network had not given the station a chance to make the changes it had demanded.

I saw my world sinking. I had left a good job in Detroit and moved my family hundreds of miles. I'd only been on the job two weeks and it looked like the rug was being pulled out from under me.

In those days we didn't have cable and satellite, so you needed one of the three networks, ABC, NBC, or CBS, to feed in national and world events.

The general manager assured me that, despite the appearance of disaster, everything was fine. "Don't worry," he said. "We're going to get an NBC affiliation contract."

I said, "Okay, fine. That works." *If it happens.*

A couple of weeks went by, and then NBC elected to go to channel 11 in Minneapolis, an independent station, instead of to the station where I was.

So I'm sitting in Minneapolis, the news director of a station that would no longer have a network affiliation, and I didn't even know if we were going to have a news department. It appeared I had suddenly gone from being the youngest major market news director in the country to probably being an unemployed one.

This was not good, for my family, for my career. Career? It would be past tense, over and out, if I didn't get back into the mainstream. The station would still have a news program, so it was not a disaster, but it was a disappointment, because budgets would be cut down, reducing what I could deliver.

As I said, back then you really had to have an affiliation with one of the three networks to have a competitive news program. Today, everything is fragmented and programming is everywhere.

There had to be a silver lining in this somewhere, and it soon exposed itself.

80

Unbeknownst to me, one of the biggest broadcasting consultants in the industry, Frank Magid, out of Cedar Rapids, Iowa, was consulting for Hubbard Broadcasting, which owned three stations around the country, including KSTP-TV channel 5 in Minneapolis. It was Hubbard's KSTP-TV station that had ended up with the ABC contract in the avalanche of affiliation changes.

According to Frank Magid, his research indicated that, in less than a month, I had made more positive changes at channel 9 than anything they had ever seen. People were talking about these changes, how different we were, how innovative we were, so there was starting to be a switchover to watch us. ABC had jumped the gun and left too fast.

Frank told me he went to Stanley Hubbard and said, "This kid's hot. You've got to hire him. Or at least get him out of the market."

I got a call from Hubbard, and he asked if I could meet with him.

I leaped at the chance. Hubbard Broadcasting had a sound financial position and a good reputation. If he offered me a suitable position, it would be a great opportunity. And even though I liked the station where I was working, I wanted out of the narrow newscast confines that hindered an independent station.

At the meeting, Hubbard told me that Hubbard Broadcasting owned three stations—in Minneapolis, in Albuquerque, and down in Florida. He wanted me to be director of news planning and development for all three. He also wanted me to produce a show with a new concept.

The employment package came with more money.

The show he wanted me to produce had an entertainment and news format similar to what *PM Magazine* later used.

I flew down to Florida to meet with key people, flew back, and went to work with enthusiasm.

I was doing planning and development for about a year, but I was missing the hands-on news business. Then I got a call from another consultant. He said that the Pulitzers' television station in Saint Louis was looking for a news director. The Pulitzers also owned the *St. Louis Post-Dispatch* at that time. Was I interested?

Of course I was.

They hired me for $75,000 a year. A lot of money to me, back then.

It was 1979. I was twenty-nine years old. I had changed employers five times and had moved my family to three different major metropolitan areas in three states. Both Cindi and the children handled the quick changes well. This time, we settled in Chesterfield, Missouri, which is a western suburb of Saint Louis.

I like Saint Louis—liked it then, like it today. It's got a big city feel but it has a small town, quaint atmosphere. It's got everything except an ocean—but it does have the grand Mississippi River.

It's a great town. There are many good businesses there. When we moved there, it was a huge city for major corporations, although over time they've lost a lot.

The people are superb. It's a great sports town, if you're into that. The spring and the fall are as good as any place in the world. The summers are hot and muggy, and the winters are the winters.

My three children also like the city, although my daughter

Wendy has taken an executive job in Indianapolis. At the time of this writing, I have six grandchildren.

When I went to Saint Louis to run KSDK channel 5, I came into a station that was still behind the times in terms of technology and everything else. So I came in and made some drastic changes. I changed the technical aspect of the station, the editing systems, the way we put the news on the air, the sets, the reporters, and the anchorpeople.

They gave me carte blanche and we built the station so that it stayed number one in the Saint Louis market for years. And I did it for three years.

We really brought that station from old-time television into the new era, and we put it on a foundation where it stayed one of the most competitive stations in the country and one of the strongest ABC-affiliated stations ever.

To do it, I worked anywhere from ten to twelve hours a day wherever I went, but I actually started working long before I got to the station. In those days, we weren't e-mail savvy or anything like that, but there was still a lot of prep time.

It all came out good. I loved my work, my career progress was steadily up, I was making good money, and my family really liked Saint Louis. And so did I. They are all still there, and I still consider it my home base.

But I still had itchy feet when it came to my career.

81

I stayed with KSDK channel 5 in the city by the Mississippi from 1979 to 1982, as news director.

I received the second Emmy of my career for an innovative set design that I came up with. We were just getting into video and live remotes, and I created an environment that was conducive to that, and they just went wild with it.

We then got a third Emmy for television scenic and set design.

Two significant things occurred in 1982 in Saint Louis. The most important was that my son, Jonathan, was born. The second event was that I left broadcasting.

I was thirty-two years old and had worked all the jobs in broadcasting that I set out to do up to that time. I wanted to try something different, and I got an offer I couldn't refuse. The offer was to be a public relations executive with Saint Louis powerhouse PR firm Fleishman-Hillard.

I was doing pretty damn well at the time, and I had an opportunity to go to a huge public relations company in Saint Louis. Fleishman-Hillard was looking for a television executive to work with its corporations, who really didn't know that much about the television business, television news, executive training, and the like. The television station had been sold, my contract was coming up for renewal, and it looked like a good time to make the change in careers that I had been contemplating.

It was a pretty good opportunity, and I weighed those two possibilities. I said, *Well, do I want to take another television news job and get a bigger market?* I was being courted by NBC at the time, to move to New York or to Los Angeles.

Ironically, Los Angeles would be where I ended up, but I wasn't ready to make the move. I decided, for my family, I should stay in Saint Louis. So I accepted a public relations executive's role at Fleishman-Hillard.

It was a huge emotional shift for me. I love broadcasting. I had been in it full-time since halfway through college. I missed it every day. And to be a public relations executive was a big change. I went from being an executive to being someone who was running my own little department of one but also was working on accounts for other executives. I was working with them on TV productions, satellite transmissions, media training, executive training for news conferences, corporate image consulting, and matters like that.

It was good for me career-wise, because what it gave me was a solid corporate foundation that I never had before. But I missed the speed of the hustle and bustle of radio and television.

Also, the public relations business was a more formal atmosphere, less of an open-collar, casual ambience than a television station, where things are both more hectic and more free-flowing.

It taught me how to deal with corporate executives who made multimillions of dollars a year. I worked with executives at Ralston Purina, Anheuser-Busch, Monsanto, Emerson Electric— all huge companies. And I learned a lot about business.

I also learned a lesson in politics.

I remember when Jesse Jackson was trying to strong-arm corporate America because he felt companies were not doing what they should for minorities. In some respects, he was pretty darn accurate about that, but I remember a closed-door meeting with him in the offices of Anheuser-Busch. A number of executives were there, including Anheuser-Busch's vice president of corporate affairs at the time, Wayman Smith.

Wayman was a prominent African American attorney, working for Anheuser-Busch, and a dear friend of mine. During this meeting with Jesse Jackson, we worked out a deal under which Anheuser-Busch would do some things to help the community, to assist him in helping minorities.

When we left the room, the media was outside, waiting for a statement from everybody, and Jackson changed instantly. He went into media mode. Everything we had talked about in this closed-door meeting was forgotten and he was on center stage with the media.

I exchanged looks with Wayman and we shook our heads. Jesse was being Jesse, and that's something I'll never forget.

I enjoyed working in public relations, and it gave me insights into the corporate world, but it was time to move on. After three years, I decided it was time I went into a business of my own.

I stayed with Fleishman-Hillard from 1982 to 1985, and really honed my corporate and marketing skills at the firm. The foundation I picked up working in the corporate world has stayed with me. I'm able to tap into it now, in my role at *Coast to Coast AM*, because I run the show like it's my own company, and it has paid off.

I left the firm in 1985. I was thirty-five years old and wanted to start my own business. The odyssey of entrepreneurship would lead me down some unusual paths, where I was treading in high-risk endeavors, sometimes stumbling, sometimes surging forward. A friend claims that I sometimes get myself into high-risk ventures that are a rough ride at the time. But, in retrospect, after the storms have passed and the waters are calm, even the toughest undertakings can be remembered as adventures.

82

The beginning of my "adventures" in running my own business began with video production. I was able to raise the financing to buy a company that was in financial trouble at the time. After I took it over, I increased sales, kept the overhead manageable, and got it going great guns.

The video production company developed into three different entities. One aspect was as a police training company. A former restaurant manager joined me for the project. We did training videos for police departments and security firms and were one of the first video training companies that trained police departments and security agencies all around the country. We would videotape live episodes that had occurred and prepare videos to train officers, showing what they did right, what they did wrong, and how it should have been done.

I had acquired the company from a client in exchange for production bills. When I first took it over, I thought, *What am I going to do with this thing?* I knew about production but not about the subject matter of the videos. It was going to take some quick learning to keep the business afloat. At least I knew I could produce the shows at cost.

We managed to do fine, and I ended up selling the business for a quarter of a million dollars a year later.

We also provided other training products for workers in other occupations. It was a nice little business, and I sold it to a publicly held company at the time.

Another aspect of video production was that we hired out to do corporate industrials and commercials for clients.

I also had formed a little programming division. We had a real estate television show on the air in Saint Louis called *Our House*. It was a regional TV show and was one of the first real estate shows about property for sale in the Saint Louis area. I also produced a video called *A Video Guide to Safe Babysitting*, which I sold to about four thousand schools and libraries around the country. The video taught young people how to babysit.

Another aspect of video production I was involved in was based near Universal Studios in Orlando, Florida. It delivered sports and entertainment video broadcasts to major television clients. The company provided the technical assistance to get televised sporting events delivered to homes by providing cameras, switchers, audio, the whole works. It was a mobile broadcasting station, a facility that would drive up to a stadium, work with a television crew to get programming ready, and then feed it either by high-speed broadcast lines or via satellite to companies like ESPN, which provided the programming to TV stations.

We were doing so well that I decided to use some of the cash flow to move into a big new video production facility. At the time, we had a contract to do a commercial for a major national company. Unfortunately, the night before the commercial was to be shot at our beautiful new facility, an employee decided to spend the night in the studio with a couple of girls and too much beer. The next morning, the commercial people were at our door with mothers and children to do their video shoot. The employee opened the door and the businesspeople saw empty beer bottles.

Of course, I lost the client, and I had to let the employee go—that day!

With a good cash flow from the sports and video production businesses coming in, I decided to enter another venture: the restaurant business.

83

Remember what I said about disaster being an "adventure" after you look back at it? Well, Indiana Jones would probably say it's only an adventure if you survive, which is something to keep in mind when deciding to change gears and go into something you have never dealt with before.

In 1987, there was a small restaurant in Brentwood, a Saint Louis suburb, not too far from my production studio. It was in the Joseph H. White Building on Brentwood Avenue. I used to eat there. I found out they were having trouble and wanted to sell. And I thought why not buy it and try my hand at something totally different than anything I had experienced? Bottom line, going into the restaurant business sounded exciting—almost like an adventure . . .

"Exciting," of course, turns out to be an understatement when you decide to go into the restaurant business. This is true at any time, but it's especially true if, like me, you already have other irons in the fire. "Chaotic" is another way to describe it. But I thought it would be an interesting business. And it was that, for sure.

So I cut a deal and set out to change the restaurant—radically. I changed the interior design, menu, and theme. About the only thing that didn't change was the physical location.

It became Café Marrakesh and Oasis Bar. Like the name, it had an exotic theme. The atmosphere of the place was based upon the exploits of Colonel William Berry, an adventurous English soldier who opened the establishment following an exciting secret mission to the thousand-year-old fortified city of Marrakesh in the Moroccan desert.

All right, I admit that Colonel Berry and his exploits were a tall tale, but customers loved the unusual dishes and the exotic desert atmosphere because we put both imagination and money into creating it. We even had the bar personnel and waitstaff dress in safari outfits.

The restaurant took off like a rocket. The first month, we did $65,000 in sales. For a small restaurant, that was huge. I mean, I thought I was on my way in the restaurant business. It was absolutely incredible.

Then the luck of the draw dealt the café a bad hand—not with the food, not with the staff, but with the parking.

When we opened, patrons would pull up to the front and drop their cars with valets, because the parking lot was behind the building and about three football fields away. But that changed when the city had to widen Brentwood Avenue to accommodate a galleria. The changes made it difficult to do valet parking.

I tried improvising, putting a golf cart at the parking lot. We called the cart the Marrakesh Express. People would park their cars and get chauffeured to the restaurant on the cart, but it wasn't the same as pulling up in front and stepping into the restaurant.

Our business dropped by two-thirds when the valet service got cut off. It was a nightmare.

They say a restaurant will live or die after a year. This one lasted a year.

One of the important points I learned about the restaurant business is that it's not a toy. That pretty much goes for about any business, but it is especially important when it's a service business dishing out fresh food and drinks. You need to be there, and I wasn't. I had a lot going on, including the video business, which I was making money at and pumping into the restaurant. I lost about four hundred thousand dollars on Café Marrakesh. That's a lot of money today—and of course it was even more back in the eighties.

I'm the kind of guy who just likes projects. I've always got to be doing something, and I generally delegate and move on to the next project. That's just who I am. Some have been ultra-successful, some have not. That's also who I am.

I also learn from my mistakes.

So now here I was. It was 1988. I was thirty-eight years old. I had left an executive position in broadcasting to assume an executive position at a public relations powerhouse. I had left the corporate world to start video production companies and had made a nice profit on each of them. I took a shot at creating and running an exotic restaurant but found that I couldn't keep it going with a golf cart.

There were a great many sensible, reasonable things that a person my age and with my experiences could do.

I decided not to do any of those things.

Instead, I chose to tackle the sport of kings.

Another adventure?

84

Horses eat and eat and . . .

All my life I have loved harness racehorses. Those are the horses where the driver sits behind them in a sulky—a small, lightweight, two-wheeled, one-horse carriage—rather than in a saddle on the horse's back.

I had gotten exposed to harness racing when I worked in Detroit. About six or seven of us got together and put in about a thousand dollars apiece and we bought a horse. And we raced him.

I just loved it. It was in my blood. So I bought a couple horses when I had my video production company going, and they did okay. They paid for themselves and I made a little money with them. But that wasn't enough for me. Despite the loss on the restaurant, I had made money and was looking for another business.

I guess if I turned to horse racing, it meant that what I was really looking for was another adventure. And I got it.

Illiopolis is a village in Sangamon County, Illinois. Population about nine hundred. It's in central Illinois, between Springfield and Decatur, a couple hundred miles south of Chicago. Some people would call it in the middle of nowhere, but it's a great place to grow things—even racehorses.

I got an opportunity to buy a repossessed horse farm near Illiopolis, a 114-acre facility that was fully equipped with a nice house, outbuildings, and a racetrack. I had the great idea of keeping the horses I had owned and breeding them, whether they were the studs or the female racehorses. I believed this would be a great little business if I could keep it going. So I bought this farm at repo from a bank, for $250,000.

I hired a couple of people, a man and woman training team, bought another little house right across the street from the 114-acre estate, and put the trainers in there. Then I started buying horses to breed. And I learned all about racehorses. I learned the lineage and the bloodlines and how to breed one horse to another to get the best out of it.

We started doing pretty good. Horses I had bred went on to earn two and three hundred thousand dollars each in their careers.

Of course, no one's perfect at judging horseflesh all the time, and we did miss a doozy.

At one point, we had seventy-two horses on the farm— mares, fillies, babies. The secret was that you had to cull them out. You had to make the necessary cuts because, as I said, horses eat and eat and eat. You had to get rid of the ones that weren't valuable as breeders or racers, but I was particular about who I'd sell to. I would not sell the horses to meat vendors who would kill and butcher them and ship their meat to places like France, where horse meat was desired.

So I always tried to find people who just wanted a horse. And the horses I was selling were not very valuable. A nonperforming racehorse could sell for from two hundred dollars to maybe seven hundred fifty, tops.

As soon as the trainer said *This one has potential* or *This one doesn't*, you made up your mind to act and sell the ones that were not capable of performing.

We had a horse called Oliver Slim. I had named him that. We didn't believe Oliver Slim would amount to anything. Along comes a young guy and offers five hundred bucks for the horse. We took it and gave him Oliver Slim.

The horse was a yearling. Horses are raced when they are two, three, four, five, six years old, but they start when they're two years old.

After training Oliver Slim, the young guy started putting him in races.

Oliver Slim won *five hundred thousand dollars* during the first two years. For a *five hundred dollar investment*. Unbelievable.

Despite the bad call on Oliver Slim—and the fact horses eat and eat and eat—we were doing okay with the farm. But I had itchy feet again.

The problem with raising racehorses is that it's a two- or three-year plan, at the minimum, and one of my weaknesses has always been that I get bored with long-range financial planning.

I've always been creative, I've always been able to set up businesses, I've always been able to make money. My problem has always been how to sustain certain things, as I had to do with the restaurant, with the video company, and with the horse farm.

The horse farm needed more capital to sustain it, to get enough horses racing and running to start paying for the facility, and I was running out of money and patience, so I had to sell that. And I did okay. I bought the house for two fifty, sold it for three sixty. Today, I suspect it would be worth two or three million dollars, because the price of acreage has gone up tremendously.

I also sold off the horses and the breeding stock and paid off my notes, so all the bankers got paid. It was a dream I love. But I didn't have the financial plan in place to really sustain myself as long as I had to.

It was now 1994. I was forty-four years old and had just gotten out of the business of raising racehorses.

I needed a backup plan.

I didn't have one.

85

In addition to my corporate career and my several business ventures after I left broadcasting in 1982, my personal life also went through transitions as the years quickly went by.

In 1987, Cindi and I ended our seventeen-year marriage.

We had started dating in high school, when she was seventeen and I was eighteen. We married when she was nineteen and I was twenty. We stayed married for seventeen years. She was the only person I had ever dated back then, and eventually we drifted apart emotionally as our interests grew in different directions.

I think that, marrying so young, the odds can be against you. People tend to marry much later today than they did in my parents' time, and that can be good. It helps people get their lives more sorted out before they have to deal with what seems to be constant turmoil, in terms of family life and careers, in our fast-moving society.

The union gave us many wonderful years, three terrific kids, and, so far, six grandchildren.

Cindi is a truly wonderful person and we have remained friends.

I got remarried, for eleven years, to another wonderful person, Lisa Trostel, who also has remained a dear friend, even after we parted.

I have to admit that a lifestyle of working nights and long hours put a real strain on my relationships. It can cause a couple to drift apart, and it makes the partner feel lonely.

By 1994–1995, I had left behind careers in broadcast management, the corporate arena, and several ventures as a business owner and operator. I was now about in my midforties and I had to figure out what I wanted to do with my life. And this time I didn't have a fallback position.

Then I saw a movie that changed everything.

86

"I want everything I ever saw in the movies!"

That line is shouted by Gene Wilder in Mel Brooks's 1967 classic dark comedy *The Producers*. But it's not that movie or that line that directly affected my life. The one that inspired me was another movie, in another era. I'll get to that, but I do love Wilder's line, and it is relevant to my situation because I was ultimately inspired by a movie.

I think most of us are like the Gene Wilder character in *The Producers*—it's hard to be human and have an imagination and goals and not want some of the wonderful things we see in movies. Especially in movies with happy endings.

I sold the last of my business ventures, the racehorse farm, in 1994.

I had had a good run, in terms of careers, since leaving my job as a television news director twelve years earlier. But now I didn't know what I wanted to do—didn't know what I wanted to be when I grew up, I guess. I just knew that I didn't want to take any of the roads I had taken before and that I needed to regroup.

Everything seemed to have suddenly fallen apart in my life, financially, emotionally. At the time, it seemed that everything just started crumbling around me after I got out of broadcasting and public relations.

I had a difficult time trying to regenerate myself, to find myself, to decide what I wanted to do for a living. I was at an age when most people have already spent a couple decades working and progressing at a job in which they are well established.

Being in your forties is pretty darn young, in one sense—it's too young to retire on your laurels. But it is also too old to go back to the bottom, start out as a copy boy, and spend years pulling yourself up the ladder.

I needed to sit back and reflect for a bit, and that's what I did. I had gone through this period where I was an entrepreneur, and I had all these incredible skills. I had learned very well that some things just didn't work.

So I said to myself, *Okay, you know what you're good at; you know what you can do. Let's take some time, regroup, and figure out what you want to do.*

So for nearly two years I did that. I tried to decide what I wanted to do. I had enough money left over from the sale of my businesses, and I just pondered what was I going to do for the rest of my life.

One night I was at home watching an Oliver Stone movie on television called *Talk Radio*, with Eric Bogosian (who, along with Tad Savinar, also wrote the play that the movie is based upon). Bogosian played the part of a caustic radio talk show host in Dallas, Texas.

I'll avoid giving you spoilers about the film, but I was watching this and I was riveted—not only by the movie and Eric's performance but also by the concept of talk radio, which I had never done before. I've been a broadcast producer and an executive; I've been a news reporter, a news manager, and a young gofer copy boy; but I've never been a talk radio host.

I was watching this in the early part of 1996, after I'd had about eighteen months to reflect on what I wanted to do, and it just dawned on me. That's what I wanted to do. It hit me like a brick.

I wanted to do talk radio. I wanted to be the person behind the microphone, not the one directing the action.

I think it's an ambition that had been incubating in me since I was a kid playing announcer and going on stage in school plays. My true love was to be an actor, but life has its twists and turns. Now I was ready to take center stage.

To achieve that goal, I started to use all the skills I had developed, the skills of running a business, the skills of being a successful producer for television, the skill of being a news guy, the skill of a media expert.

I decided to reformulate myself and reconstruct myself.

Before we get to that, though, let me explain a little bit about talk radio itself.

87

Broadcast radio has been around for about a hundred years, and talk radio has been there for most of that time. One of the first successful talk radio hosts was evangelist Aimee Semple McPherson. McPherson not only had a highly rated show in the early 1920s but also eventually owned her own radio station.

Politics, religion, and local, national, and world news—it has all been around for a long time. Even shows at night investigating the paranormal. The first major dark-of-night paranormal-themed host was a guy named Long John Nebel, who got his moniker because he was tall and skinny.

During the 1950s, radio had lost a great deal of its audience to that phenomenon called television and was looking around for a way to interest an audience. Along came Nebel, an auctioneer, whose contact with radio had been only as an advertiser, not as an entertainer. He talked a New York station into giving him a talk show and they gave him the midnight to 5:30 A.M. slot, the graveyard shift, when most people were asleep.

For more than twenty years, from the mid-1950s to 1978, when he passed away, Nebel's popular talk show explored the supernatural, the paranormal, the unusual, and about everything that was unexplainable.

Radio broadcasting features a built-in delay, whereby a host can prevent profanity, threats, or other outrageous comments from going out on the air. Nebel's station, fearful that his telephone callers might utter swear words, created a seven-second delay. An engineer named Russell Tinklepaugh invented the process.

On my show, today, we have an even longer delay to ensure that profanity isn't broadcast.

On May 15, 1993, *Coast to Coast AM* with Art Bell was launched to a nationwide audience by Chancellor Broadcasting Company, under the leadership of Alan Corbeth. A Ku-band satellite uplink was installed at Art's home in Pahrump, Nevada, so Art didn't have to commute to flagship station KDWN in Las Vegas, more than an hour away, to do the broadcast each night.

88

I wanted to be behind the microphone. The big question was how I would I get there.

I was in Saint Louis. I didn't want to move. That narrowed the geography but severely limited the opportunities.

The next question was who would want to hire me as a talk show host? For sure, I had had successful careers in broadcasting, but not behind the mic, despite my early experience as a radio reporter. Reporting didn't actually count because you don't have to make it up as you go along (as Indiana Jones claimed he was doing in *Raiders of the Lost Ark*).

How do I get back into radio when I had done it many years before, in a different context? How do I go to a radio station executive and say that, since the last time I was behind a radio mic, I've been a television producer and a public relations executive, have run a production company, have owned a restaurant, have raised racehorses that eat and eat and . . .

You get the idea.

Having been an executive in television myself, I know that if somebody had come to me and said, *Look, I want to be a TV reporter but I have no experience doing it*, I would have said, *Hey, go to a smaller market, work for five years, come back and show me a tape.*

Well, I didn't have that kind of time. And I didn't have an inclination to go to another small market. I had been in Detroit, in Minneapolis, in Saint Louis. I was recruited to go to New York, to Los Angeles, and to some smaller markets.

As I started to put this plan together, with the idea of what I wanted to do, karma stepped in.

KMOX radio, which is a strong CBS-owned station in Saint Louis, rated number one, was raided by a fellow who put together an investment group and bought a station in Illinois. It was a five-thousand-watt station, and his idea was to use the station to springboard to being the next KMOX in Saint Louis.

The man's name was Tim Dorsey. Dorsey hired many of the people from KMOX, who, for whatever reason, left the number one station. I can only imagine that he must have offered them one sweet deal.

So they bailed, and that left KMOX shorthanded.

I saw this as an opportunity. I was getting ready to go into talk radio—I wanted to get into something—so I called the program director, Tom Langmyer. I said, "Tom, I want to do talk radio. This is George Noory." He knew of me because of the market, and I told him, "I'm ready to do this."

He said, "Well, can you be here tomorrow to meet me?"

I said, "Yeah, sure."

So I went by and met him and his news director, John Butler, and things just worked out. They said, *Look, we could use you. We're going to hire you part-time; we'll pay you this per hour. We can use you to do talk news.*

It was a talk format, and they needed me to fill-in on late night talk shows. I was hired to cover for people who were sick, on vacation, or otherwise unavailable. It meant putting on a different hat every night—sometimes several times a night. We'd start there and see what happened.

So, in 1996, that's what I started doing. I was the fill-in guy at KMOX. I did fill-in talk radio at night, I did news during the day, I did my own show with a coanchor on

Saturday mornings called *Total Information*, and it was kind of fun.

I wasn't getting rich but I was paying the bills, and I was building that experience and that exposure.

Then karma stepped in again.

Show host George Noory listens with the same respectful tone he uses whether callers have Ph.D.s in microbiology or advanced degrees in wacko. . . .

Noory combines the unexplained with something unexpected—in-depth chats with some of today's most respected scientists.

—Randy Dotinga, "*Coast to Coast AM* Is No Wack Job," *Wired* (February 15, 2006)

89

Tim Dorsey had bought another strong five-thousand-watt station in Saint Louis, called KTRS. He brought everybody over from WIBV, the station he already owned, which he then sold to Disney. Then KTRS became a talk station.

Now, he's listening to me through fill-in, and they're running shows, including *Coast to Coast AM* at midnight. He contacts me and says, *How would you like to do your own talk show, late night, twelve o'clock to four or five in the morning? I'll pay you [not a lot of money], but it will be your show.* He said he was going to drop *Coast to Coast* with Art Bell.

And I said, "Sure, I'd love it."

So that was my next entrée into how things worked out.

I'd been fill-in for KMOX for a year and then, all of a sudden, on Labor Day 1997, I started the *Nighthawk* show in Saint Louis.

The Nighthawk, that's what I called myself. It just was great for me. Except for one thing: the *Coast to Coast* fans weren't getting that show anymore. Instead, they were getting this new guy on the air. Some people had heard me on KMOX, but a lot of people had not. And they're calling up on my talk show, screaming, thinking I'd dumped *Coast to Coast*.

It took a couple of weeks for them to lighten up a little bit and start liking me, and they started understanding: *Hey, you know what? This is pretty good. This is great.*

Even before I got my own show, I'd actually been doing shows on UFOs, ghosts, and other supernatural topics, despite advice that it would negatively affect my career. I did them back when I was at KMOX, filling in for talk show hosts like Jim White, who has since passed away.

Tom Langmyer, the program director, called me into his office one day and said, "George, you're doing a great job for us, but do me a favor: drop the supernatural stuff. There's no future for you doing that."

Uh-huh. He stills brings that up whenever we bump into each other.

So I started doing my local show called *Nighthawk*. It was a talk radio show, except I was doing most of the talking. I didn't get any phone calls. People weren't calling in to do the thing that keeps a show moving—talking.

So I started playing the song "Where Have All the Flowers Gone?" by Peter, Paul, and Mary, and every time the word *flowers* came up, I powered the song down and yelled, "Phone calls!" So it would go, "Where have all the *phone calls* gone, long time passing? Where have all the *phone calls* gone, long time ago?"

I'd power it back up again, then again power down, and I'd take out "flowers" and put in "phone calls." People started calling. One guy called and said, "Hey, what would stop you from playing that?"

I said, "Don't hang up. Stay on the line with me."

One caller became two, became three, and ultimately my show became a very successful, highly rated program.

So I was doing fill-in; doing my show midnight to five A.M., Monday through Friday and on Sunday. Then I got word that Art Bell had decided to retire. He was on a different Saint Louis station than me at that time but was syndicated nationally.

All of a sudden, a friend of mine, Mike Siegel, was chosen to replace Art Bell. Mike was doing some work for us on KTRS in Saint Louis. He lived in Seattle and we would hook him up via high-speed ISDN lines and Mike would do a show for us every once in a while during the daytime.

I had gotten to know Mike, and so I called him up. I said, "Mike, you've replaced Art Bell. This is huge."

He said, "Yeah, I've got to study the format. I'm not into this stuff. But, yeah, I got it."

I said, "Mike, do me a favor. I'm sending you a tape. Give it to the guy who's in charge of *Coast to Coast*. I want to back you." He said, "Yeah, sure thing."

He got the tape and he sent it to the guy but I never did any backup until the affiliate went from four hundred stations to 333. (We're at six hundred now.)

The network cut a deal to get Art Bell back on, after one of his many retirements. So they let Siegel go after about a year and Art was back, doing the show on a different station than me in the Saint Louis market.

I was doing mine at midnight, competing with him, and I was killing him in the ratings.

Well, one day Art's back started falling apart again, and that guy that Mike had given the tape to needed someone to back Art up. He had listened to my tape and realized that I did many of the same things locally that they did on *Coast to Coast*. I had UFO shows and other strange things like that.

Alan Corbeth, the guy in charge of Premiere Radio, which carried Art Bell in Saint Louis, called me out of the blue and said, "Look, I need you to start filling in for Art. Would you do it?"

It's no problem doing a national show from Saint Louis. The broadcasting network is set up so that I could have done the show from any of the hundreds of radio stations in the country that carried it.

So, in April 2001, they cut me a deal that I'd fill-in nationally from Saint Louis and still keep my own show. For each *Coast to Coast* show, I'd be paid an amount that was astronomically higher than what I was making doing the local show.

Things were great. I was doing my own show and up to

three shows a week for Art, as his back starting getting worse and worse.

I did this for about six months.

Then, one day, the station that I was competing against in Saint Louis, which carried my own *Nighthawk* show, called Corbeth and said, "You do know the guy is killing us locally in the ratings. Why are you having him fill-in for Art?"

He said, "He's the best one for it." And they said, "No. That's a no-no."

It went all the way up to the top brass, and they decided I wasn't going to fill-in any more.

I was crushed. I was absolutely crushed. Talk about depression.

Goldberg: I know you've been doing this for eleven years. Why are you drawn into this?

Noory: Since I was a little boy I was into the paranormal, the unusual, the strange. I started doing *Coast to Coast* and I get phone calls from real people. . . .

Here's an example. A police officer calls me and says, "George, you're not going to believe this. We got a call about a person who was having a heart attack in a house. We were the first responders. We got there before the EMTs got there. We get there, we knock on the door, a little old man opens the door. We come in, we look on the floor, and there's a guy there on the floor. We roll him over. He's dead. It's the guy who opened the door for us." He turns around, the guy is gone.

This happens time and time again. It's unbelievable.

—Interview with Whoopi Goldberg,
The View (September 18, 2013)

90

So, for about a month, no more *Coast to Coast* shows. Then one day Dorsey called me into his office and said, "Look, I'm taking you off midnight to five."

I said, "Why?"

He said, "We're moving you up to six-thirty to midnight."

I said, "Wow, that's five and a half hours." That's a long time, but it's more prime time for me. It meant more money. They had given me a deal where I could sell my own commercials, so I was making more that way than being paid a straight salary.

He says, "I got even better news for you. I'm bringing *Coast to Coast* back and they've agreed to let you fill-in again."

I went, *This is amazing, absolutely amazing.* And that's what I started doing, for a long, long time.

I was doing my own show, and eventually Dorsey gave me just nine to midnight, so I could have more of a life. So I was doing that, nine to midnight, and filling in for Bell two or three days a week, from midnight until four or five in the morning, as Art's health got worse. After I signed off my show at midnight, I would just run down to another studio, and it would be my little *Coast to Coast* hook-in studio. But there was a catch: I didn't always know whether I was going on the air for Art.

It worked like this: I'd finish my show and get down the hall, in position to do *Coast to Coast.* Then I would wait, not knowing if I would hear Art's voice. If I heard Art's voice, I would get up and leave. If I didn't hear Art, I'd start talking.

Things were going so good that something had to put the skids on it.

Soon Dorsey called me into his office and said he needed to take some commercial time away from me, that I was making too much money.

That commercial time was three minutes an hour on my show that I was permitted to market to businesses. The deal resulted in me getting a decent return on the show without burdening the station.

I said, "Wait a minute. We had a deal, and the deal was I get three minutes an hour, and I can sell them and do whatever I want and get the money."

He said, "I'd like to cut that back down to two."

I stood my ground and he backed off.

At the time, I was angry enough to think of quitting, but I thought, *No, I want the* Coast to Coast *job. I know one day Art Bell is going to retire, and I will be at the right place at the right time.* Keep in mind that in the time I had been filling in for Art, I had never turned down a request.

My efforts paid off.

In September of 2002 I got a call from the network. They told me that Art was going to quit, effective the first day of 2003. And they offered me the full-time job of hosting *Coast to Coast AM.*

Their representatives flew to Saint Louis and met me at the Ritz-Carlton. They had a contract with them.

To paraphrase an elderly Italian gentleman from another movie, they made me an offer I couldn't refuse.

It was a done deal.

PART XI

COAST TO COAST AM

91

In September 2002, I signed the contract to become the host of *Coast to Coast AM*, with a start date of January 1, 2003. On that first day of 2003, I made my first broadcast as the full-time host of the show. It was a Wednesday.

I wasn't in Pahrump, Nevada, where Art had broadcasted from.

Nor was I in Los Angeles, where Premiere Networks is headquartered.

I was in Saint Louis, not running down the hallways to get from one studio to another but in my own studio. And I like Saint Louis, so that was fine when I started doing the show full-time. But I quickly decided that my best foot forward would be broadcasting from Los Angeles. I had been filling in on the show off and on for a couple of years, but I always did it from Saint Louis. I'd decided that it would be better if I broadcast out of L.A. for a while, too, to work with the people there.

I didn't want to be just a voice that they heard. To do even better than I had been doing, the people I worked with needed to deal with me in person. That meant I had to be physically present at Premiere's Sherman Oaks headquarters, so that's why I decided to do the show in Los Angeles.

I called up my network president, Kraig Kitchin, and a little good karma starts again. Kraig says, "We'd love to have you in Los Angeles." So he rewrote my contract, gave me more money.

As I've said, I like Saint Louis. I have children there. So I just kept going back and forth between the Los Angeles and

Saint Louis studios, which is what I continue to do today, in addition to some other "home bases" I've acquired.

There is a backstory to Kraig Kitchin and me. It's one of those *life can be strange* kind of stories.

When I was a producer in Detroit, back in 1975, 1976, one of my newspeople was a guy named Ken Thomas. Ken had had polio, walked with a cane, wore glasses, and was a sharp dresser. He was our anchor guy and I was his producer. He was a sharp, brash newsman.

Ken would sometimes bring a little boy into the studio with him, his son. Every once in a while he would show his son around, and then he would take the boy home and come back and do his six o'clock or eleven o'clock newscast with me. And that went on for about a year or so before Ken left.

Fast-forward about a quarter century or more. I was in Premiere's Sherman Oaks office talking to Kraig Kitchin. I saw a picture on his desk and recognized the person in it.

I pointed at the picture and said, "You know, I worked with a guy in Saint Louis whose television news name was Ken Thomas, but his real name was Ken Kitchin. He bears a resemblance to you."

Kraig started tearing up.

I said Ken used to walk with a cane.

Kraig said nobody knew that his father walked with a cane.

I said, "Kraig, you were that little boy, weren't you?" Of course he said yes.

It just changed the complexity of everything we do—then and in the future. At the point I'm writing this, Kraig Kitchin, who's no longer network president, is my agent. He handles Rush Limbaugh, me, and many others.

A PERSON WHO WAS THERE

I'm Tom Danheiser, the senior producer for *Coast to Coast AM*. I've known and worked with George since the day he took over the show.

I often think back to the day when we all gathered in Sherman Oaks, California, where Premiere Networks is located, so he could meet his new L.A.-based team. The group gathered in one of the conference rooms in the building and everyone's energy was on high in anticipation of meeting the new host of *Coast to Coast AM*.

So in walks this man with an incredibly good aura about him, and with a smile and personality that anyone would be accepting of.

I immediately liked him!

George spoke to us and talked about how excited he was to be there to meet everyone, and how he looked forward to working with us on this humongous talk show called *Coast to Coast AM*.

After addressing the collective room, he then went on to talk individually to us. When he got to me, I shook his hand.

I remember chatting with him and learning that we had a few things in common, including scuba diving, and of course the love of radio.

It didn't take me long afterward to discover yet another thing in common: George genuinely cares about human beings, as I do.

Well, that was a lot of years ago, and since then we have

gone on to have more than just a working relationship . . .
George became and remains my friend!

His persona on the radio is the same as off the radio; a
genuine, nice guy.

Over the years, I have seen, time and time again, George
help people in numerous ways. This includes me. I remember George lending me his car once. Now, I know this
seems like a little thing, but believe me, not having a car in
L.A. is like not having a paddle in a table tennis match!

George is one of the good guys!

92

So that's how I got my own show and then moved on to the *Coast to Coast AM* arena. There were ups and downs along the way; some fun times, like running a restaurant and raising racehorses; and some expensive lessons in life and in business—like running a restaurant and raising racehorses who eat and eat and . . .

I'm still going strong, and we've branched out. I'm doing television programs, have been in a few movies, and have an Internet show.

Even though I came out and got behind the mic in Los Angeles, I really haven't "moved" there. I stay in Los Angeles and do my shows there when I'm in town, but I'm also "based" in Saint Louis, Dallas, and Hawaii as well. So I'm just all over the map. I think the gypsy-like DNA that I got from my wandering ancestors, which kept me changing jobs, cities, and states after I left college, is still keeping me on the move.

I've been asked if going national and international with *Coast to Coast AM* has changed my perspective of broadcasting. It hasn't. The feeling that I had on January 1, 2003, is the same feeling that I have today. It has never changed. In my mind, I broadcast to one person, one listener, and I don't go off the beaten path on that.

I have never, ever, thought of myself as this huge syndicated talk show host. It's strange for me. When I walk through airports, appear at speaking engagements or other events, or otherwise go out in public and people come up to me and say, "Aren't you George Noory?" and they're aghast, it still has a strange feeling to me. To this day I have remained just me. That *Night-hawk* broadcaster from Saint Louis just happens to have a bigger role today, and I just go with the flow.

One thing, for certain, that has never changed goes back to my youth. I have always been curious about everything. That curiosity has taken me to all kinds of places, including places that nobody else goes. Sometimes even where nobody should want to go.

I keep constantly busy, either on the move or doing the show. The schedule consumes most of my life during any given month, and that would include the radio show, the television show, weekend speaking events, live shows that I do—about 80 percent of my life revolves around that.

My prep time for the radio show starts just about the minute I wake up. Even when I'm working out on a treadmill I've got my smartphone and I'm texting people and taking phone calls about the show or about the TV show.

I have looked at *Coast to Coast* as my own business, and one of the things I think the network likes about me is that I look at it not just as a radio show but as an enterprise that has revenue, has employees, has production people, and has an amazing audience. I have taken it under my wing and make sure that I'm involved in each area of the program—marketing, publicity, airtime, commercials, everything.

93

I've been on the move most of my life. Changing careers and houses, moving to different towns, changing states many times. It started as soon as I was married. In short order we had gone from an apartment to a suburban house and then to a farm way out in the countryside. And the energetic movement continued as we went from Michigan to Minnesota and Missouri.

As I've said, maybe having predecessors who wandered in search of home and peace has given me wanderlust in my own blood.

My stint in Saint Louis was my longest run anywhere as an adult, and that worked out well because both my family and I liked Saint Louis and my late night *Nighthawk* show had been both a kick and a hit. Saint Louis is a big metro area, millions strong, and even though there are only a few cobblestone streets and antebellum buildings left, the city has a musical soul—jazz, blues, and ragtime—that makes it a little South, a little North, and a lot in between.

Now I was at it again, and this time it was the biggest change in my life in terms of geography and career. But it also involved something deeper than where I lived and what my job was. My psyche and my soul were to be tested by a new job in a new environment.

It is almost a couple thousand miles from Saint Louis to Los Angeles, but the difference is more than the number of mileposts in between.

Up to the time I took over the helm at *Coast to Coast AM*,

I had lived my entire life in the Midwest. I had had opportunities that would have taken me to either coast, but I had always found that my career prospects and lifestyle for my family were just as good or better in the Midwest. Now my kids were adults and had their own lives and I had what I considered to be the opportunity of my lifetime: going national and international with a paranormal show of my own.

There was no question that I had to do it. If there was anything that would make me leave a town I liked, and my old show, it would be taking the new show national. I had to take Horace Greeley's advice, pack my bags and head west, leaving a lot behind—but taking a lot with me, too.

Fortunately, I was in a financial position where I didn't have to cut all ties to Saint Louis. My children were well settled there, and I knew I could keep up the family ties not just by phone but also by making Saint Louis a second place where I hang my hat. Ultimately I would add Hawaii to the places I call home, and I grew familiar with cities I traveled to frequently as I became a busy guest and moderator for events.

Did I feel like I had won the lottery? In a way, I suppose it's that feeling of exhilaration when something significant and exciting happens in one's life. There is always an element of the luck of the draw in life, whether it's the incredibly fortunate near miss when stepping off a street corner as a truck roars by or being in the right place, at the right time, for a career opportunity.

As with most people whom providence has suddenly smiled upon, my change from being behind a regional mic to going coast to coast and beyond was preceded by decades of hard work, a lot of sweat, and maybe even a few tears as I occasionally crashed and burned while venturing into new territories.

I had no regrets about those years that led up to starting over again in Los Angeles. I liked most of the jobs I ever had, even when I burned bridges on the world I knew and took a risk to try new things.

Today, I think of having had a restaurant and a horse ranch as "adventures," even though at the time when the road department was putting my exotic café out of business or horses were eating me out of house and home, the situations felt more like nightmares.

Coming to Los Angeles and taking on a show with the largest audience I had ever broadcasted to on a regular basis was going to be a challenge—but I hoped it would not be a nightmare.

What could go wrong?

First, there was the town itself. I've lived in metro areas that have millions of people, but the Los Angeles region, with nearly twenty million people sprawled over an area about the size of Indiana, has an annoying distinction: it has no taxis and little mass transit. There are great restaurants, wonderful places, even a downtown with grand old movie palaces but that is like most downtowns—if you don't work there, there's little chance you're going to visit it often. The downside to L.A. is that the only way to get to anywhere is by car. It is a car town—no walking permitted!

Los Angeles didn't turn out to be that much of a culture shock or culture collision for me, despite my Midwest roots. I love diversity, and L.A. is about as diverse as any city can get. Besides one hell of a lot of concrete and asphalt, capped off with beautiful beaches and great weather and bad air, there are people here from every place on Earth, and not a few that are from far beyond . . .

One of the fortunate things about Los Angeles is that it's composed of a lot of smaller parts. The headquarters and broadcasting studios for my show are on Ventura Boulevard in Sherman Oaks, an area that lies on the north side of the Santa

Monica Mountains, which are mostly only a couple thousand feet high. On the south side of the mountains are Hollywood, Beverly Hills, Bel Air, and West Los Angeles. Spread out on the north side is the San Fernando Valley.

Premiere Networks, the largest syndicator of radio programs in the world, syndicates *Coast to Coast AM* and many other high-profile names and shows. *Coast to Coast AM* is broadcast to more than six hundred radio stations. We reach all fifty states, plus Canada, Guam, the Virgin Islands, and Sirius XM Satellite Radio, channel 146.

Was there pressure in taking over the show? Of course there was. Not that I had that much to learn. I had spent most of my adult life in broadcasting, had had my own talk show, and was enthralled with the paranormal, so I knew the territory. But even though I knew the ropes, there was pressure from a different angle: Would Art Bell's audience accept me?

I had stood in for other talk show hosts many times. I had been standing in occasionally for Art Bell over the years, before he retired and I was offered the job. But Art was a trailblazer and I knew he was going to be a hard act to follow. Radio talk show audiences, like fans everywhere, tend to be very loyal and even somewhat zealous. Because it was an ongoing show, I would be stepping in with a different cadence than Art's audience had been experiencing.

But I brought with me to the show years of experience and a determination to throw everything I had into it. And the effort worked.

I think one of the reasons I've been successful doing the show is that I learned from my tremendous failures as a business owner. I made some pretty wild moves, and not all of them worked. But I did learn. And I run *Coast to Coast* as if it's my own company.

I meet with the salespeople regularly. I'm watching the financials. I have my eye on the strategy and direction of the show, alongside my executive producer, Lisa Lyon, who was in the studio, line producing my very first night as a fill-in host for *Coast to Coast AM*, and is one of the most brilliant minds working in talk radio today.

In a sense, it has become my business.

I think the mistakes I made in the past—and I made many—really have helped me to where I am today.

YOUR BELIEFS ARE WHAT IS IMPORTANT

"People will call me and ask me, what do you believe? And my answer to them is, one, it doesn't matter what I believe. It matters what you believe. And that's what I try to do with the program. Whether I'm interviewing someone on a hard news topic or something else, I try not to inject my views into it. I'm kind of old school broadcasting, where I would rather have the public decide for themselves, rather than have something force-fed from me. So they don't know. They don't know if I believe in UFOs. They don't know if I believe in ghosts. They don't know if I believe in God. I have my own reasons, and my own views, believe me. But by and large, I try to stay out of it. I try to be more of a facilitator, rather than a dictator."

—Stefene Russell, "A Conversation with
George Noory," *St. Louis Magazine*
(January 25, 2013)

94

I told you I'm mad as hell and I'm not going to take it anymore. None of us should take it.

I stopped taking it quite a while ago, when I stopped thinking of myself as an entertainer who has to keep an audience interested for four hours most nights of the week and started viewing myself as a facilitator who can communicate to millions of people—not just about what problems our nation and society suffer but also about a possible path to get solutions into the hands of those who can make things happen.

A point I made early on is that the world has been changing under our feet. There is no longer a long-term, generational effect in which the world changes at a slow but steady pace over a person's lifetime. Looking at what has happened during the past several decades, it is clear that business, government, schools, medical services, the news and entertainment media, and just about everything else about our society, including the way we fight and define war and peace, have changed and are still changing and transforming, even as I write these words and you read them.

The metamorphic changes and the inability of our legal, business, and political systems to smooth these processes have left many people feeling helpless, frustrated, and angry. And why shouldn't it? There seems to be no end to the malfeasance and even denseness of our political leaders, who yap endlessly at each other, pandering to this or that special interest group, even as they get richer at our expense and play the fiddle while Rome burns.

The worst thing about our political leaders is not that they are stupid—some are extremely bright. *It's that they just don't care.* And sometimes I wonder if it's because they don't understand.

Politics not only has become a game for the superrich, with campaigns running into tens and even hundreds of millions of dollars, but also, like business ownership, it has grown more and more dynastic, with child following parent. That nepotism frequently comes along with so much wealth that the individual who wants to lead our state or nation has little idea about what the average person really needs in terms of necessities like income and medical needs.

No wonder the wealth gap that is destroying the most productive people in our society is completely out of control.

Along with incompetence at every level of government and public schools that have lost touch with how parents need and want their children to be educated, there are movies full of sex and mindless gory violence, not to mention comic strip characters, produced in a steady stream from Hollywood.

Add endless wars that seem to have no beginning, no end, and no rational purpose and that seem to pop out of nowhere.

The dangers are not that far away, either. Someone joked to me that they don't go to movies, malls, or schools for fear of getting shot. Sad to say, it's not funny.

Mass murder committed by "ordinary" people has been called a uniquely American phenomenon, although the rest of the world seems to be adopting the madness.

What kind of society have we evolved into, where we have to fear for the safety of our children at schools—or where the violence and terror in a movie theater could exceed that of what's on the screen?

We have enough sick crazies intent on harming innocent people in our own country that, in and of itself, it's a type of "homegrown terrorism." It doesn't matter that their only ideological statement is that they have gone off their medication or they want to avenge some slight at work, in love, by their family, or that they just have a desire to murder others as payback for the miserable lives they brought on themselves.

Add the fact there has been an assault on faith of every kind and an attack on our liberties that is unprecedented in modern times in our country. Some of that assault has to do with the fact that political correctness has grown to the point that even ordinary people fear what they say, because a private Facebook or other Internet entry can go viral. Your sudden fifteen minutes of fame can be scorn and insults thrown on you by thousands of people around the world because you expressed a private opinion or what you said is misconstrued.

I've told you that I see the state of the world, the global instability that threatens our own nation's stability, as part of a deliberate, systematic process of undermining our nation in an attempt to weaken it. One can only imagine what would happen to this world, in short order, if the United States was not capable of keeping the forces of evil and the Dark Ages from overwhelming the world.

What would happen if we lost our ability and freedom to fight evil and instead come under the controlling tentacles of a world government that is dancing to a tune played by secret hands? It's not hard to imagine that the forces of evil would rise and overwhelm the world because the only country with the ability and determination to maintain peace and order was disabled.

No wonder people are dazed. All the world's problems are in our faces and our homes, with the advent of the Internet. Not only does the Web bring the bad into our homes but also the ease of global travel brings many negative things, along with the good, into our towns and cities. All that exposure to what is happening everywhere, all the time, makes it difficult for many people to get a grip on things.

One fundamental "wrong" in our society hits right at home, literally, and that is the war against the middle class. I call it a war because there appears to be a determined effort to financially and emotionally assault large numbers of people who are struggling to achieve and keep even the most basic features of the American dream they are entitled to share. We know that an unprecedented number of young people are stuck at home or are dependent upon their parents because they have been squeezed economically out of society, but the young need to know that even the older generations are being squeezed.

From my own family history, I know that it is no fantasy that, when baby boomers were conceived, there were some common things that most Americans expected. That included ownership of a home with a modest mortgage and the hope of paying it off, and a couple of affordable cars in the garage. There was little credit debt, families took vacations, people were more important in medical and dental offices than the plastic card they carried, and most people had a little money set aside for an emergency.

Of course, most large companies had something called a "pension" for people who spent most of their adult lives at their jobs.

I don't need to tell you that those things are all gone with the winds of change.

It didn't disappear overnight, but over years, stealthily, due to bad leadership in our government and people in our business world so greedy that we scoff at the term *millionaire* because billionaires have become so common. While middle-class people struggle to provide an education and opportunities for their children, and their grown children struggle to pay their own way, there are houses and works of art that sell for more than a hundred million dollars.

Today, a large number of hardworking people often can't afford to buy a home, and if they are able to manage it, the taxes, insurance, maintenance, and a never-ending mortgage can chain them financially to the house, keeping them from saving money for retirement (no pension offered!), taking a vacation, or owning cars with odometers that aren't approaching—or exceeding—the six-digit mark.

Add to this our leaders ignoring killer asteroids, potential power grid disasters, the Internet of Everything Wrong, and we know there are a great many things we need to address before we suffer irreparable harm.

Most of all, we have to remind ourselves that our lives have value.

And sometimes we need to get mad.

I'M AS MAD AS HELL!

"I want you to get mad . . . You've got to say, 'I'm a human being . . . My life has value.' So I want you to get up now. I want all of you to get up out of your chairs. I want you to get up right now and go to the window, open it, and stick your head out and yell, *'I'm as mad as hell, and I'm not going to take this anymore!'*"

—Howard Beale, *Network* (1976)

(emphasis added)

95

I've spoken about how a drive toward "interconnectedness" that links us all together through the Internet and other technology weakens us in many ways. A good example is the fact we are so connected, not just nationally but *individually*, to the power grid and everything that it delivers to us—and it is already delivering ever so more as the Internet of Things grows. This represents "control" over us, because what it gives can be taken away in a flash, leaving chaos in its wake, putting us back a century or more, taking us from the tech age to the tool age.

Interconnectedness also links us together to control what we see and hear and, ultimately, what we think and do. When we are all connected, the Internet becomes a weapon of control of our thoughts and beliefs, and ultimately our actions, by those unseen hands pulling the strings of global manipulation.

But that interconnectedness that we are doomed to be corralled into also has a positive effect for those of us willing to use it. Like Paul Revere racing down city streets shouting a warning, our radio, television, and Internet mediums permit us to band together to educate ourselves and to deliver warnings about lazy politicians and the dark forces of biblical proportions that seek control and conquest.

It is my belief that unless we—*we, the people!*—wake up and take control of our destiny, defeating the forces that subvert our faith and erode our financial security, we will lose our freedoms of thought and action.

I've said I see myself as a facilitator, that my program being broadcast coast to coast for hours at a time is both a listening post to keep me informed and a way for me to get out my sense of what is coming down.

For those of you who care and are willing to help—and I think that most Americans instinctively have that attitude—you can get mad! Stay informed! Put out to others the word about what you've learned! Let your opinions be known!

Remember how God cleansed Earth with a flood? That's what we need to combat the problems of society—only, in this case, we need a flood of popular opinion and support for laws and regulations that support the common good. A flood of votes for positive change in the ballot box. Votes for those politicians who are capable and are willing to implement change for the common good.

Keep aware of what matters to you. Vote intelligently.

Most of all, we need to stay informed. It doesn't matter whether it's wars, weather, water, the destruction of the middle class, the power grid, killer asteroids, or suitcase nukes, we all need to stay informed and get the word out to the powers that be, when we see our leaders ignoring problems, acting stupid, or more likely getting their opinions from lobbyists who write them checks.

The most important thing is for all of us to keep up our spirits, even when we see things are not going well, either personally or with the country.

We need to stay calm in an electrified world that sometimes seems to be sizzling with madness, electrified insanity that ignites in quick flashes like lightning, hitting here and then there, death and destruction following the social thunderstorms—so much so that we cannot deal with them emotionally.

But do get mad in a positive way. It's okay to be angry and to demonstrate your opinion in positive ways, rather than falling into a state of gloom and doom as the obstacles seem overwhelming. Obviously, getting mad and going into a rage adds to rather than diminishes the problems confronting us.

I mentioned earlier that there is something I call a "wireless Internet," which connects all of us, and that I seem to have a router in my head. What I am seeing from those concepts that come to me is that good people are being assaulted on all levels. Machinations, manipulations, mindless acts of war and terror, clandestine climate engineering—all with felonious intent, crimes of premeditation.

I can see that strings are being pulled and that our politicians often dance like puppets, with their hands out for "campaign contributions" and their minds shut to the needs of the people they represent.

It is happening at all levels of government, at the highest levels of corporate America.

There are facts that I can prove with solid evidence and others that I can infer from what I see but that need more proof.

There are names I am not ready to state until all the evidence is in.

Until then, I will be waiting, listening, keeping my mind open and clear.

I have been called a voice in the darkness.

That is where you will find me when you need me.